Dick Francis

RECOGNITIONS

Mystery Writers

Bruce Cassiday, General Editor

Raymond Chandler by Jerry Speir
P. D. James by Norma Siebenheller
John D. MacDonald by David Geherin
*Victorian Masters of Mystery: From Wilkie Collins
to Conan Doyle*
by Audrey Peterson
Ross Macdonald by Jerry Speir
The Murder Mystique: Crime Writers on Their Art
edited by Lucy Freeman
*Roots of Detection: The Art of Deduction
before Sherlock Holmes*
edited by Bruce Cassiday
Dorothy L. Sayers by Dawson Gaillard
Sons of Sam Spade: The Private Eye Novel in the 70s
by David Geherin
*Murder in the Millions: Erle Stanley Gardner—
Mickey Spillane—Ian Fleming*
by J. Kenneth Van Dover
Rex Stout by David R. Anderson
Dashiell Hammett by Dennis Dooley
The American Private Eye: The Image in Fiction by David Geherin
John le Carré by Peter Lewis
13 Mistresses of Murder by Elaine Budd
*The Secret of the Stratemeyer Syndicate: Nancy Drew,
The Hardy Boys, and The Million Dollar Fiction Factory*
by Carol Billman

Dick Francis

Melvyn Barnes

The Ungar Publishing Company/New York

Copyright © 1986 by The Ungar Publishing Company.
Printed in the United States of America

Library of Congress Cataloging-in-Publication Data

Barnes, Melvyn P.
  Dick Francis.

  (Recognitions)
  Bibliography: p.
  Includes index.
  1. Francis, Dick—Criticism and interpretation.
2. Detective and mystery stories, English—History and
criticism. 3. Crime and criminals in literature.
4. Horse-racing in literature. I. Title. II. Series.
PR6056.R27Z59   1986   823'.914   86-6997
ISBN 0-8044-2011-4
ISBN 0-8044-6023-X (pbk.)

Contents

Starter's Orders

Dick Francis was responsible for my highly antisocial behavior at Christmas 1974. Some twelve years after its original publication I had acquired a paperback of his first novel *Dead Cert* and, oblivious to the calls of the festive season and more importantly to my family responsibilities, I read it from cover to cover.

My introduction to Francis's fiction therefore came quite late, at a time when there were twelve other novels already enticingly available. Having savored their delights, and those of every subsequent title, I find the readability of Francis's work remains as compulsive in my case as it was on that (in some respects) unfortunate Christmas Day. His worldwide sales are sufficient indication that I am not alone.

It is not merely the sheer entertainment value of Francis that prompts this volume. He has other gifts that ought to be recognized, and that require a full-length study if justice is to be done. His mastery of pace and suspense is universally acknowledged, but attention needs also to be paid to the skill of his characterization, the messages and themes he conveys, and the quality of the writing itself. The creation of superla-

tive thrillers for his readers is achievement enough, but the
fact remains that he offers so much more. That said, it must
be emphasized that this study is not to be a pretentious affair
seeking to ascribe deep meaning and profound psychological
significance to his books. Dick Francis, a modest man, would
doubtless be amused to be so treated.

After a brief introduction and a biographical summary,
the following chapters analyze every Francis novel published
to date. Chapter 10 presents an overall assessment of his fiction, and the many features that have secured him a place as
an international novelist of distinction. Numbered notes and
references are not elaborated as footnotes in the text, but are
collected in the separate notes section where they appear nu-
merically in relation to each chapter. The volume concludes
with a bibliography of material by and about Dick Francis,
and an index.

Every effort has been made throughout to avoid the practice of revealing plot details, to the extent that they spoil the
enjoyment of those who have yet to read the novels themselves. While the fact that Francis is not a writer of "whodun-
its" makes this danger less likely, my analyses of his stories
will inevitably inform some readers of points they might prefer to acquire for themselves by reading the novels first. I am
confident, however, that such indiscretions have been kept to
a minimum.

For the provision of materials or information that assisted
me in my research, my gratitude goes to the staff of West-
minster City Libraries, the City of London Libraries, and the
United States Information Service in London, and also to Pro-
fessor Paul McCarthy of Lawrence, Kansas. Finally I record
my warmest thanks to Dick Francis, and to his agent Andrew
Hewson of John Johnson Limited, for the considerable help
they have given me in the preparation of this book. The time
they have so generously devoted to my inquiries is deeply
appreciated.

Form Book

This biocritical study covers the first twenty-two novels by Dick Francis. He has recently added *Proof* and *Break In* to his list, and continues to display the fine qualities examined in detail here. His short stories are not considered here, but will be found listed in the bibliography at the end of this book. His popular appeal may be judged from the fact that all his novels are still in print in hardback and paperback in the United Kingdom, as are many in the United States; they have been translated into eighteen languages, and his world sales figures exceed twenty million copies.

Francis has thus enjoyed great success with the reading public. So too have many other crime and adventure novelists, but Francis's distinction lies in his inclusion in that comparatively small band of popular novelists who have also been widely acclaimed by the critics. Purely within the crime fiction field he has been highly honored, the recipient of three Edgar Allan Poe awards by the Mystery Writers of America (for *Forfeit*, *Whip Hand*, and *Reflex*) and the Silver Dagger and Gold Dagger awards by the Crime Writers' Association (for *For Kicks* and *Whip Hand* respectively). It is also evident, however, that he has become increasingly regarded as a general novelist of quality, rather than as a genre writer who has achieved the breakthrough by acquiring the critics' rather grudging seal of approval.

It is worth looking back at this point, and marveling a little, at how all this started. When Francis wrote *Dead Cert* a few years after his retirement from steeplechasing, it was for purely financial reasons. Heywood Hale Broun has commented upon the probable limitations of Francis's horizons at the time: "When he took up fiction he probably did not aspire to more than the mantle of Nat Gould, a competent hack whose turf tales gave reading pleasure to men who'd grown too old for the *Boys' Own Paper*. On good days . . . Francis might have dreamed of equalling Edgar Wallace."[1] In terms of sales and their reputations as first-rate storytellers, Gould and Wallace would not have been bad writers to emulate; but Francis, as it later transpired, had more to offer than an entertaining yarn. He also possessed the literary ability to attract the attention of those who would never have expressed an interest in the work of those earlier masters of the racing mystery.

But would Francis produce more novels with his specialist background? And would they not inevitably become stale and fall into a set formula? These were the obvious questions that arose when Francis the jockey became Francis the writer. Julian Symons, eminent historian of crime fiction, had little doubt when he reflected many years later: "It seemed unlikely that his specialised knowledge would provide more than three or four fictional themes. Mr. Francis has proved those who nursed such thoughts to be entirely wrong. He has varied his plots intelligently."[2] Francis has indeed used his experience in the racing world to produce a number of interesting and ingenious bases for some of his plots, while in others he has bravely pushed racing further into the background and concentrated his attention upon alternative subjects. What could not have been foreseen at the outset, but is now quite clear, is that each of his novels stems from its central character. If the racing background had been the prime factor, perhaps he would unavoidably have become a formula writer; but with his central character as the prime factor, his versatility has been unlimited and quite independent of his racing knowledge. This will be seen in the analyses of the individual novels in chapters 2 through 9.

It is difficult to place Francis in the context of crime fiction or to identify him with one particular school or style. As a writer of racing thrillers he could be compared with Nat Gould or Edgar Wallace, but his literary standard and his explorations of positive themes and character motivation put him on a higher plane. He has possibly derived something from his friend John Welcome, another writer of what might be described as racing thrillers, but it would be more accurate to classify Welcome's novels as sophisticated espionage tales where high life, motorized pursuits, and glamorous women are of greater significance than characterization or even than horse racing. Francis himself dislikes the label "racing thrillers." "I consider my books to be adventure stories rather than thrillers," he says, and cites Desmond Bagley, Gavin Lyall, and Alistair Maclean among the authors with whom he would be happy to have his style associated. Although not an adventure novelist, Ed McBain is another contemporary author whom Francis admires.[3] All these writers, it should be noted, use the crisp and economical technique favored by Francis; they do not waste words if to do so would be to retard the action or impair the readability.

There are elements of Francis's works, including his essential Britishness and his recurrent portraits of the lone hero pursued by villains, that inspired Timothy Foote to assert that "he belongs in the company of writers like John Buchan."[4]

Francis, in an interview with Alistair Burnet, only vaguely recalled that he had read Buchan but had clearer recollections of Edgar Wallace and Ian Fleming, supposing that "their way of writing implanted itself in the back of my mind."[5]

It is with Ian Fleming that Francis has been frequently compared, sometimes by prominent scholars of literature and to Francis's advantage. C. P. Snow has remarked upon Francis's "considerable inventiveness, both in plot and in technical devices, so that on the superficial levels his books would compare favourably with the James Bond stories."[6] Philip Larkin has referred to Francis's best features in greater detail, itemizing "the absolute sureness of his settings, the freshness of his characters, the terrifying climaxes of violence, the literate jauntiness of style, the unfailing intelligent compassion," and concluding that "all these make him one of the few writers who can be mentioned in the same breath as Fleming."[7] Snow nevertheless believed Francis to be superior in terms of his readability, tautness, and lack of pretentiousness, and saw greater similarities with the early work of the sadly neglected Nigel Balchin. This might be an idiosyncratic view, but it is undoubtedly more fruitful to look for parallels with such writers as Fleming and Balchin than to group Francis with the writers of "racing thrillers" or "sports mysteries." Psychological drama and the conflict between good and evil are salient points of comparison, as is the theme of the lonely protagonist who is motivated to behave in a particular fashion by certain influences, pressures, and obsessions. Taking the latter point, Jessica Mann has mentioned Francis in passing when considering the work of Geoffrey Household.[8]

Two further quotations may be examined to find the essence of Francis. His novels, asserts Michael N. Stanton, "concern violence, fear, greed, and virtue in the world of horse racing. . . . Within the limited ground Francis has claimed for himself, he has found room for exquisite variations of setting, plot, and psychology."[9] Edward Zuckerman concisely sees Francis as having created "a world of admirable horses, despicable villains and ordinary men called upon to be heroes."[10] By overlooking Stanton's qualifying phrase "in the world of horse racing," it is then easy to see the wide scope Francis has given himself and the opportunities he has taken to explore "exquisite variations": the novels are indeed about violence, fear, greed, and virtue, irrespective of setting. Zuckerman's perceptive implication about the conflicts felt by Francis's ordinary men is an important facet of every Francis story, but the admirable horses have had a decreasingly important role to play.

Francis's versatility has come through, in spite of the frustrations that could so easily have been caused by readers who seemed always to expect a strong horse-racing element. He has proved himself to be an excellent novelist rather than a fictionalizer of the specialized world he knows best, and could effortlessly produce a first-class thriller or adventure story with no racing connection whatsoever if he chose to do so, but it is unlikely that there will ever be such a Francis novel. "I doubt," he says, "if my regular readers would want it or accept it."[11] Perhaps he has chosen the wisest and most satisfying course of action, expanding his horizons by almost surreptitiously easing racing out of the limelight in most of his later books and introducing other subjects and backgrounds. To various technical fields he has now given prominence, fascinating rather than disappointing his readers by providing them—and himself—with the best of all possible worlds.

In the latest edition of his autobiography, Francis refers to the plateaus upon which the more fortunate writers find themselves. He has, he feels, reached three such plateaus.[12] When questioned about this statement, he says that the first plateau was for him the significant action of writing, the actual beginning of a new career when he put pen to paper; the second, after a few books, was the general agreement that his works were well received and that he was no longer regarded

as a former jockey indulging in a sideline; the third, which
came with the publication of *Whip Hand* and the release of
the television series *The Racing Game*, was the achievement
of major success and recognition, not only at home but internationally.[13]

The next plateau for Francis will conceivably be his acceptance as a significant novelist, and he is one of the few
writers of popular fiction today who could achieve this without turning to the "mainstream novel." The value and intelligence of his writing should be recognized, irrespective of the
fact that he chooses to work in the thriller form. Edward
Zuckerman quotes Phyllis E. Grann of G. P. Putnam's Sons,
Francis's New York publishers: "I always took Dick Francis as
a serious writer. . . . I always read him as a really excellent
novelist who happened to use the thriller form."[14] While it is
devoutly to be wished that critics would take a similarly en-
lightened attitude, this whole debate is immaterial to Francis
himself; he is delighted that people of all ages tell him that
they enjoy his books, particularly youngsters who will be the
readers of the future, and he has little time for self-aggran-
dizement.

Even when viewed simply as a popular novelist, Francis
is frequently regarded as being head and shoulders above
most of his contemporaries. In a rather unkind (to others) review of a recent Francis title, Michael M. Thomas asserted
that "At a time when thriller-writing is dominated by the pretentious, lugubrious pap of the Robert Ludlums of this world,
it's more than being tossed a life-preserver; it's like being of-
fered the *QE2*."[15] Similarly John Mortimer, celebrated man
of letters, is prepared to accept Francis at his face value and
declare him to be excellent: "Mr. Francis's work might be said
to be perfect holiday reading. . . . He has the magical power
of making you forget the sunburn and the mosquito bites, the
gyppy tummy and the sickly smell of Ambre Solaire mixed
with frying calamaris."[16]

It is a constant source of complaint by crime writers that their work receives scant attention from the critics. Why, they ask, can distinction not be recognized in those novelists who happen to be specially accomplished in one genre? Why, they have asked from time immemorial, must they turn to mainstream fiction in order to be deemed respectable? Raymond Chandler found the problem irksome as long ago as 1949: "The sort of semi-literate educated people one meets nowadays . . . are always saying to me, more or less, 'You write so well I should think you would do a serious novel.' You would probably insult them by remarking that the artistic gap between a really good mystery and the best serious novel of the last ten years is hardly measurable compared with the gap between the serious novel and any representative piece of Attic literature from the Fourth Century B.C."[17] The question of the critical recognition of crime writers remains to this day, although Dick Francis is among the few who have received more serious attention than would have been forthcoming a few years ago. He is a good example of a popular novelist who displays no self-indulgence, writing for his readers rather than for himself, which should surely be no reason for failing to acknowledge that he writes extremely well.

Francis, then, is a phenomenally successful writer who has recently been given the consideration normally denied to popular novelists as a class. It is fully warranted. His scope is not limited by the racing background he has adopted to a varying extent throughout his books, nor is his imaginative or literary ability hindered by the fact that he chooses to create thrillers or adventure stories. Two comments emphasizing these very points are worth repeating here; the first relies upon exaggeration for its effect but is eminently quotable, while the second comes from a superlative scholar/practitioner of The Novel. "Not to read Dick Francis because you don't like horses," said John Leonard, "is like not reading Dostoevsky because you don't like God."[18] "In many respects," said C. P. Snow, "his books are deeper than so much work which we dignify, often fooled in this Alexandrian climate, by the name of Art."[19]

1

The Hero as Himself

It is fortunate indeed that Dick Francis has written his autobiography,[1] which originally appeared in the United Kingdom before he turned his attention to fiction. It provides not only an invaluable insight into a steeplechasing career that gave him the essential background to his novels, but no reader can fail to identify in it his generosity and humility, his lucidity, and his sense of humor. The picture revealed is that of a man whose character and personality is far removed from the mean world of violence and deception so often presented in his novels, but in style it is as compulsively readable and crisply presented as anything he has written. As with most of the heroes he has introduced to the reading public, what communicates itself is firmness and fairness in all things, together with an essential likability. The existence of his own fascinating account therefore means that only a brief biographical summary is required here.

Richard Stanley Francis was born on October 31, 1920, at Tenby, in the Welsh county of Pembrokeshire. He was educated at Maidenhead County Boys' School in Berkshire, although he makes no secret of the fact that his studies suffered in competition with the abiding interest of his life—horses. This is hardly surprising, since his father Vincent Francis was first a professional steeplechase jockey and later manager of the reputable W. J. Smith's hunting stables at Holyport near Maidenhead. Riding was in the family tradition, and the young Dick spent extensive periods on the Pembrokeshire farm of his grandfather.

Dick's lack of enthusiasm for school did not lead to rebuke by his family. Clearly they could themselves appreciate his greater attraction toward an outdoor life, pursuing what he saw as "more exciting things . . . going on outside, in the absorbing world of men."[2] His hours in the stables, and particularly in judging the likely potential of the foals, enhanced his feeling for horses, their behavior, and their performance, which was to prove significant for both of his professional careers many years later.

As Dick's riding improved, so he was exhorted to even greater efforts by his father. This strong paternal influence, which carried with it the implication that he was never good enough and must try harder, has been mentioned by some commentators in referring to the autocratic father figures suffered by some of the heroes in his novels. His autobiography, however, shows that his own father was more a firm and positive influence than the bombastic and humiliating fathers of his fiction, against whom his heroes usually rebel. In Dick he instilled determination, skill, and courage on horseback, and these qualities appear also in the gritty protagonists of his novels.

Dick's passion to become a steeplechase jockey was not to be fulfilled for many years. The ambition of this young man, as of so many others, was temporarily thwarted by the outbreak of World War II. Having signed on as an airframe fitter with the Royal Air Force in 1940, he gave further evidence of his dogged will and his search for action by making repeated applications to train as a pilot. Persistence led to success, and he spent much of the war flying fighters and bombers. Immediately after his initial training he was able to identify a quality in flying that was to him enjoyable. "In solo flying," he says, "I found again what Service life denies, the blessed peace of being alone."[3] It might not be too fanciful to see in this picture the lone hero with great responsibility in his hands, the model for so many of his later fictional creations.

Shortly after the war ended Dick Francis met Mary Brenchley, the woman who was to become his wife. To their respective families it was not at the time the ideal match. Mary, with her university education, was not engrossed in the world of horses and it was unexpected that she should decide to marry a man who wanted to become a jockey. A courtship combined with mucking-out stables and cleaning the leather in tack rooms is hardly a romantic picture, but Dick and Mary were compatible from the start and horses were to be the dominant feature in their life together.

While working as a farmer-trainer's secretary and dealing with accounts, and in spite of parental warnings that being a jockey was a financially uncertain and dangerous occupation, Dick Francis rode his first steeplechase as an amateur at the comparatively late age of twenty-five. On May 3, 1947, after thirty-nine races, he had his first win on Wrenbury Tiger at Bangor-on-Dee. Later that same afternoon he won again on Blitz Boy, and by the end of the season he had ridden nine winners. The season concluded with the sort of catastrophe that jockeys seem to accept with equanimity; a broken collar-bone resulted in his wearing a sling at his wedding (somehow symbolic!) the following week.

In his second season he began to win on Rompworthy, a partnership that finally produced thirteen victories. He was asked to ride in most of the principal chases for amateurs, and his autobiography details his rapidly developing experience and his assimilation of racing lore and tricks of the trade. Not

only are the latter described in the manner that enlivens his
narrative, but he was to remember these many small points
and use them to good effect in his first novel *Dead Cert*. The
verisimilitude of his fiction was to rely heavily upon the in-
sights he gained some years earlier into the innumerable
wrinkles of race tactics and techniques.

Dick Francis was an amateur National Hunt jockey from
1946 to 1948, then rode as a professional until his retirement
in 1957. An early breakthrough was the opportunity to ride
for Lord Bicester, one of the greatest names in National Hunt
racing, who gave him the chance to experience his first Grand
National; this was in 1949, when his mount Roimond came
second. His consolation was to win the Welsh National shortly
afterwards, on Fighting Line for the Ken Cundell stables.

The tragedy of Dick Francis's life at this time was that his
wife Mary contracted infantile paralysis, and was confined to
an artificial respirator. He describes his feelings after visiting
her in the hospital: "My mind was filled with the image of
Mary as I had just left her, with only her head free of the grey-
painted wooden box which enclosed her body while a big
electric bellows pumped air in and out of her lungs. I stood
trembling and shaking, and . . . I found I was uncontrollably
crying."[4] Mercifully Mary recovered, but the horror of that
time and for the many months while the danger remained left
a vivid impression upon Dick. Later he was to write with
compassion about James Tyrone in *Forfeit*, a man whose wife
has suffered identically but who knows that recovery is out of
the question.

Disease and disablement in the domestic situation is
something with which even the toughest man can find it difficult to cope. In contrast a steeplechase jockey learns to live
with the many injuries he might himself expect to receive in
the course of a career. The tally of Dick Francis, by the time
of his retirement, was twelve broken collarbones, five broken
noses, innumerable broken ribs, three crushed vertebrae,

breakages of arms and wrists, a fractured skull, and a damaged spleen. The fact that all this is taken in a professional's stride, often with a short recovery period and little interruption to his racing, is a partial answer to those critics who complain that Francis's fictional heroes absorb physical punishment with too little effect. "Because of his hard fitness," says Francis, "the effect his injuries have on him should not be judged by the effect they would have on an average man."[5]

The 1953–54 season was memorable for Dick Francis. He was invited to ride for Peter Cazalet, the Royal trainer; he also built his own house near Blewbury, on the edge of the Berkshire Downs; and he became Champion Jockey, with seventy-six wins. This, his greatest season, ended with the fulfillment of his dream to visit the United States. Much later he was able to make effective use of the information gained on the American racing scene and in sightseeing—for example, in *Blood Sport.*

One ambition only remained, to win the Grand National. Like so many steeplechase jockeys of high quality, he was to end his career still lacking this coveted prize. He rode in the Grand National eight times, but unlike any other jockey he is still remembered for one of those occasions on which he did not win. "A post-mortem one day may find the words 'Devon Loch' engraved on my heart,"[6] he says, referring to the calamity that befell him in the 1956 Grand National on the Queen Mother's horse. With a mere thirty yards to the winning post, and with a lead of some ten lengths, Devon Loch unaccountably collapsed.

Dick Francis's spectacular exit from the 1956 Grand National remains steeplechasing's classic upset, and is still a mystery. The *Liverpool Daily Post* described it at the time as the greatest tragedy in the history of the sport, and nobody has yet produced a universally accepted explanation. There was no injury to Devon Loch; theories have ranged from heart attack to muscular spasm, but the most widely believed idea is that the horse tried to rise to a nonexistent obstacle, a "ghost jump." Naturally Francis devotes considerable space to the Devon Loch incident in his autobiography, and it is reasonable to accept that he is the expert and was in a better position to observe Devon Loch's behavior than all those who subsequently produced innumerable column inches on the affair. He describes with great effectiveness the shock wave of sound that came from a crowd of 250,000, all cheering home the winner and its owner, possibly the most beloved woman in the world. It was this incredible noise, he believes, that caused Devon Loch to react nervously, interrupting the rhythm of his stride and bringing him to the ground.

Soon after this, which was Francis's last Grand National, history strangely repeated itself. He won the Welsh National, just as he had done after his first Grand National in 1949. Crudwell, his 1956 winner, also gave him his very last win at Leicester in January 1957.

Dick Francis's career as a professional jockey ended in February 1957. He retired, after much heart-searching and with great regret, while he was still at the top. He had ridden some of the greatest horses, and had won 345 of his 2,305 races.

It is not surprising that such a well-known figure found himself in demand. He accepted jobs as an official judge and as a race commentator but, more significantly as it later transpired, he agreed to write a series of articles for the London *Sunday Express*. This was extended to a long spell as racing correspondent for the newspaper from 1957 to 1973, to which discipline he attributes the economy of style so evident in his fiction, and which also provided him with an awareness of the workings of Fleet Street he put to such excellent use in his novel *Forfeit*. His central character James Tyrone, like Francis a racing columnist, displayed apprehensions that must have been felt by Francis himself on many occasions. When interviewing a Steward of the National Hunt Committee, Tyrone senses his wariness:

I saw that uneasy expression almost every day of my life: the screen my racing friends erected when they weren't sure what I was after, the barrier that kept their secrets from publication. I didn't mind that sort of withdrawal. Understood it. Sympathized. And never printed anything private, if I could help it. There was a very fine edge to be walked when one's friends were one's raw material.[7]

The sensational Devon Loch incident had prompted literary agent John Johnson to suggest that Francis should write his autobiography. This he started before his retirement, and on its publication in London in December 1957 *The Sport of Queens* was immediately successful. Francis the writer, who wrote nothing until he was thirty-six years old and who confesses that he still finds it difficult to put pen to paper, was on the threshold of a brilliant second career.

His first novel *Dead Cert* was written for financial reasons when he needed a new carpet, repairs to his car, and the wherewithal to educate two sons. It has given rise to twenty-three successors, translations, serializations, radio plays, a television series, and a movie. If awards by the Crime Writers' Association and the Mystery Writers of America may be used as a yardstick, he has produced novels of quality.

"Looking back to the 1956 Grand National," says Francis, "so much that has happened since that day seems incredible. One is forced to wonder how much would have been the same if Devon Loch had won that race; and, in honesty, I think I owe more to his collapse than I might have to his victory."[8] He still regards his steeplechasing years as the best years of his life, and it is unlikely that even now he has overcome the feeling he passed on to his hero Sid Halley in *Odds Against* and *Whip Hand*, the memory of exhilarating wins and the realization that it will never happen again.

Dick and Mary Francis still live in their purpose-built Blewbury house with its fifty-four acres of farmland, although they spend the winter months at their apartment in Florida's Fort Lauderdale. Mary is his indispensable researcher and critic, while their two sons (one a trainer, the other a teacher of physics) are also active in providing specialized information to give added authenticity to his novels.

When asked if he prefers to be considered as jockey or writer, Dick Francis continues modestly to think with greater pride of his racing years but can appreciate the different kind of success he now enjoys. "Success as a writer is more enduring," he says, "whereas success as a jockey is immediate and ephemeral. When you win a race everyone is cheering and back-slapping, but soon afterwards it's all over and they are wondering about your next race. The popularity of a novel lasts longer. It's also nicer to be thought of not only as that chap who *didn't* win the Grand National."[9]

On March 20, 1984, at Buckingham Palace, Dick Francis was invested as an Officer of the Most Excellent Order of the British Empire (OBE). Her Majesty The Queen and Her Majesty Queen Elizabeth The Queen Mother no doubt remember him with gracious affection as "that chap who didn't win the Grand National," but it is equally certain that they know him also as a writer who has brought great distinction to the world of the British thriller.

2

The Hero as Jockey, Hate Object, and Spy
Dead Cert
Nerve
For Kicks

Dick Francis's first novel, *Dead Cert*, appeared in the United Kingdom in 1962 and was well received.

> The mingled smells of hot horse and cold river mist filled my nostrils. I could hear only the swish and thud of galloping hooves and the occasional sharp click of horse-shoes striking against each other. Behind me, strung out, rode a group of men dressed like myself in white silk breeches and harlequin jerseys, and in front, his body vividly red and green against the pale curtain of fog, one solitary rider steadied his horse to jump the birch fence stretching blackly across his path.[1]

These opening words not only show Francis's ability to engage the reader's interest from the first page with a few crisp and well-chosen words, but in retrospect they can be seen as heralding a brilliant career; a second brilliant career, no less, and drawing upon the experiences of the first in fine style. It was probably not obvious in 1962, but he was to go from strength to strength and to show increasing skill and maturity, often with something to say in addition to providing good entertainment. He was also to find it unnecessary to rely completely upon the fascination of the turf as the mainspring of his popularity, and today his ability to set this in perspective with other themes and backgrounds has enhanced rather than diminished the acclaim with which his books are received.

The narrator of *Dead Cert*, Alan York, is a young steeplechase jockey with all the passion and competitiveness that Francis displayed himself. As the enthusiastic sportsman, the talented amateur among the hard-bitten professionals, it would be strange if Alan York were not a reflection of Francis in his younger days. All twenty-four Francis novels to date are told in the first person, and while he has undoubtedly used his narrators to convey his own attitudes, emotions, and morality, it is in Alan York that we see the least complicated example of the author-protagonist-hero with a fervor to jump fences and win races, the fighter who remains a gentleman. His single-mindedness of purpose and his raison d'être are disturbed only by the aggressive actions of criminals, resulting in the defensive and retaliatory responses that turn Francis's books from fictional autobiographies to enthralling thrillers.

Dead Cert opens with calamity, when Bill Davidson's mount Admiral falls at a fence at Maidenhead. Admiral, the "dead cert," or certain winner, has lost his first race in two years. It is little consolation to Alan York to win the race as a result of the accident, because it is obvious to him that his close friend Bill has been very seriously injured. Alan, who lives with the Davidsons, is beset by nagging doubts about the cause of Bill's sickening fall. Francis conveys with feeling the subtle, irritating worry assailing Alan, when he thinks of the attendant who crossed the course as Bill approached the fatal fence, and then recollects the fleeting metallic gleam of something out of place. On inspecting the scene Alan finds a coil of wire, which he suspects was looped across the fence by the attendant when he saw Admiral approaching and then rewound immediately afterwards.

> The callousness of it awoke a slow deep anger which, though I did not then know it, was to remain with me as a spur for many weeks to come.[2]

Here for the first time appears one of Francis's motifs, the driving force of anger felt by the peaceable and honorable protagonist. In Alan York's case it reaches full force very quickly, with Bill's death in the hospital impelling him to root out and expose the people responsible. But first he sees it as his role to help the Davidson family through their grief, and Francis paints a most perceptive picture of the three young Davidson children, with their mixture of infantile emotions and determined worldliness in direct contrast to Scilla Davidson's shattered horror at her husband's death and her inability to cope with the tragedy.

It is a major responsibilty for Alan but, like many a Francis hero to come, he shows he has the mettle for it. Alan is no stranger to the need to display strength and maturity. Aged only twenty-four, he has left Southern Rhodesia to represent his father in the London office of the family company of transporters, while pursuing his own interest in steeplechasing. The pressures Francis places upon his heroes are always considerable. In this case the young Alan has not only to become a substitute for Bill, an emotional support for Scilla and the children, but he feels compelled to investigate Bill's death when the police appear loath to act. When the skepticism of Inspector Lodge (first of a long line of unfriendly Francis policemen) turns to suspicion of Alan himself, this increases the pressure and effects what has become the classic Francis transition from innocent bystander to avenging angel. The sugges-

tive questions of Inspector Lodge relating to Alan's victory in
the race as a consequence of Bill's fall, and the unpleasant in-
nuendoes about Alan's relationship with Scilla Davidson, spur
him to positive action. There is now a need to clear himself, as
well as to unravel the mystery of his friend's death.

Alan's investigation does not dominate the book. He continues to ride in races, and as the story progresses the suspense is maintained by switches of scene and mood between
the pursuit of Bill's killers and the fascinating milieu of the
racecourse. It is at the races that Alan is introduced to Kate
Ellery-Penn, who is looking for a rider for her horse Heavens
Above. The horse was a present from her Uncle George, who
with Aunt Deb has brought up Kate from the age of two. Alan
is immediately attracted to Kate, but also sees a possible
connection with Bill Davidson. He learns that Uncle George
had wanted Bill to ride Heavens Above, and in turn reacted
strangely to the news of Bill's death.

Francis clearly distinguishes between the two women,
Scilla and Kate, and Alan's feelings for them. Regardless of
police suspicions to the contrary, his love for Scilla is platonic.
For Kate he feels a strong sexual inclination, and sees in her
the qualities that Scilla lacks:

> She was a vivid, vital person. It seemed to me that she
> had an inexhaustible inner fire battened down tight under
> hatches, and only the warmth from it was allowed to es-
> cape into the amused, slow voice. Kate was going to be
> potently attractive even in middle age, I thought inconse-
> quently, and it crossed my mind that had Scilla possessed
> this springing vitality instead of her retiring, serene pas-
> siveness, Inspector Lodge's implications might not have
> been very far off the mark.[3]

In contrast Scilla presents Alan with no sexual temptation, even when she shares his bed. A combination of gruel-
ing questioning by the police, brandy, and drugs have left

her drained and wretched. Tearful and insomniac, she comes
to Alan's room in the small hours.

> I switched off the light and lay in the dark, gently cra-
> dling her until her breath grew soft and she was soundly
> asleep. . . .
> During the night Scilla twisted uneasily several times,
> murmuring jumbled words that made no sense, seeming
> to be calmed each time by my hand stroking her hair. To-
> wards morning she was quiet. I got up, wrapped her in
> the eiderdown, and carried her back to her own bed. I
> knew that if she woke in my room, with the drugs worn
> off, she would be unnecessarily ashamed and upset.
> She was still sleeping peacefully when I left her.[4]

This is a tender scene in which Francis is content with
compassion and sympathy, whereas many other writers might
be inclined to transform it into something more sensational.
Indeed the Woodfall film of *Dead Cert* (1974) did so, introducing a sexual relationship between Alan and Scilla that is
alien to Francis's intentions. The Francis heroes are men of
honor, and this is invariably seen in their attitude towards
women; while they are in all cases heterosexual, they would
never take unfair advantage of a woman, and certainly not of
the widow of a best friend in her most vulnerable hour.

While Francis has shown himself to be adept at conveying relationships between men and women when necessary, he is not a writer who deems a romantic or sex interest
to be obligatory. In *Dead Cert*, the love affair that grows between Alan and Kate is not a strong element in the plot, and
Francis studiously avoids allowing it to develop as an interruption to the main story; Kate is not really a key character,
but serves to introduce the more strongly drawn characters of
her Uncle George and Aunt Deb.

If the romantic element in Francis's fiction is often weak,
he unfailingly excels in another area. The characters of the
turf, shrewdly presented with an experienced eye and always

surrounded with the authentic atmosphere of the racecourse, are a constant delight. Whether or not they are integral to the plot, or simply a diversion to lighten the suspense before piling it on once more, they are all real people. Francis has, it seems, known and worked with versions of all of them. In *Dead Cert* they abound—the elderly Clem, the valet who "stroked a saddle as another man would a pretty girl's cheek, savouring the suppleness, the bloom";[5] glamour-boy jockey Dane Hillman; red-haired, happy-go-lucky jockey Sandy Mason; and mean and aggressive young Joe Nantwich, his career as a jockey marred by drink and dishonesty.

Here Alan York plunges "into the bustle of a normal racing day, the minor frustration of a lot of jockeys changing in a smallish space, the unprintable jokes, the laughter, the cluster of cold half-undressed men round the red-hot coke stove."[6] When old Clem hands Alan his clothes and tack, and Francis itemizes them, it is hardly fanciful to suggest that one senses the aura and smells the leather. Then later the reader experiences, in a few short paragraphs, the excitement at the opening of the Cheltenham National Hunt Festival:

> Three days of superlative racing lay ahead, and the finest 'chasers in the world crowded into the racecourse stables. Ferries from Ireland brought them across by boat and plane load; dark horses from the bogs whose supernatural turn of foot was foretold in thick mysterious brogue, and golden geldings who had already taken prizes and cups galore across the Irish Sea.
> Horse-boxes from Scotland, from Kent, from Devon, from everywhere, converged on Gloucestershire. Inside, they carried Grand National winners, champion hurdlers, all-conquering handicappers, splendid hunters: the aristocrats among jumpers.[7]

Francis also shows what motivates such men to do the things they do. While some are inspired by conceit or recklessness or the lust for fame, Alan derives his satisfaction from being his own man away from the family business. He also finds racing a strangely pleasant contrast to his background in Africa:

> The speed of racing, the quick decisions, the risks, these were what I badly needed to counteract the safeties of civilisation. One can be too secure. Adventure is good for the soul, especially for someone like me, whose father stopped counting after the fourth million.
> . . . And I, for whom the deep jungle was a familiar playground, found the challenge I needed in a tamed land, on friendly animals, in a sport hemmed all about with rules and regulations. It was very odd, when one came to consider it.[8]

The Dick Francis heroes are never presented as macho but are normally quiet, ordinary individuals, sometimes taciturn and rarely extrovert. They are basically observers of the scene around them, not involving themselves in trouble or danger (except when riding) unless it hits them head-on or they are enveloped in a situation to which they are obliged to react. It is not surprising, therefore, that Alan York is reluctant to interest himself in the affairs of the luckless Joe Nantwich, who is engaged in a feud with fellow-jockey Sandy Mason and has also incurred the ire of a racehorse owner called Clifford Tudor.

Nevertheless Alan is forced to inquire into these relationships, as various points indicate that one or all of the people concerned know something of the circumstances of Bill Davidson's death. While Tudor is uncommunicative and Mason is bantering, Joe Nantwich is garrulously the worse for drink. This is a good character sketch, with Nantwich alternately surly and maudlin, constantly blaming others for his own misfortune. He is a skillful jockey, but disliked by his colleagues because of his manner and unreliability. Francis shows him to be a pathetic example of degradation, a young man of barely twenty on a downward path instead of rising to the heights appropriate to his ability. He whiningly confesses to Alan that he has deliberately taken bribes to lose races, on the instructions of an anonymous telephone caller who is now threatening him if he fails to cooperate further.

Alan's tenacity is increased rather than diminished when he is lured into a horse box and beaten up by four men. Their intention is to dissuade him from asking further questions about Bill Davidson, but the essence of the Francis hero is that he will not be deterred by violence and intimidation. By this time even Inspector Lodge is convinced that Bill's death was no accident, but the Francis hero has already emerged from his quiet shell and Alan is motivated to pursue the matter to the bitter end.

A favorite device of Francis is to break the suspense and slow down the action, or to provide action of a different sort by taking in the races, which leaves the reader in a state of painful anticipation until the hero is suddenly and often violently thrown again into the fray. It is a masterly technique, bearing comparison with the planning and pacing all good jockeys must learn if they are to romp home in an ideal race. Just as Francis knew from long experience when to conserve the physical resources of his mount and when to surge forward, so he knows unerringly when to keep the reader on tenterhooks and when to let the action build to the next peak.

So at this juncture in *Dead Cert* he moves to Cheltenham races with Alan York, and for good measure Alan has the best win of his career. It is marred not by thoughts of Bill Davidson, but by the fact that Alan has grown away from his father —another trait, together with his appearance as something of a "loner" among the other jockeys, that was to be a recurrent feature of Francis's heroes in later books.

While at Cheltenham, Alan passes the word around the course about the trip wire and the events following Bill's "accident," in order to create a climate of antipathy towards the gang and to force them into the open. Francis conveys the image of a racecourse as a community, a quaint network where news travels fast and people stick together. The only positive result, as far as Alan is concerned, is a telephone call from a man with a husky, whispering voice. In an oblique way, for someone who professes to dislike violence, he promises that the next warning will be more painfully applied by his men if Alan persists in asking questions.

Francis continues to keep the action at low key, and acquaints the reader with his own irritation at outmoded social attitudes toward jockeys as Alan visits Kate at home and meets the imperious Aunt Deb. Her prejudice is neatly summarized:

> "Kate tells me you are a jockey, Mr. York." She said it as if it were as dubious as a criminal record. "Of course I am sure you must find it very amusing, but when I was a gel it was not considered an acceptable occupation in acquaintances."[9]

Uncle George is also described in a few choice words, reminding Alan of "so many businessmen I had met in my work, the slap-you-on-the-back, come-and-play-golf men who would ladle out the Krug '49 and caviar with one hand while they tried to take over your contracts with the other."[10]

Aunt Deb and Uncle George, very conscious of Kate's social position, probe blatantly into Alan's background and his father's occupation. In telling them that his father is a "trader," Alan is aware that this term could cover anything from a rag-and-bone merchant to the head of a large corporation. When he omits the specification that his father falls into the latter category, Alan is not only being gentlemanly in wishing to avoid embarrassment by refuting their suspicions; he also fails to see why he should parade his family's success and financial security in order to demonstrate his acceptability as a human being and as a suitable companion for Kate.

Later, in *Flying Finish*, there is the same determination in
Lord Henry Grey to prove that rank is leveled by a man's actions and that inheritance is immaterial.

Another motif favored by Francis is the retaliation of ordinary people against the threats and bullying of organized
villains. This is seen most clearly in his narrator-protagonists,
but sometimes in others. In *Dead Cert* the criminals are not
only race-fixers, but also run a fleet of cabs called Marconicars
as a cover for a protection racket that terrorizes small trades-
men in the resort town of Brighton. In a nice character cameo
Francis shows how the owner of a pub, retired Regimental
Sergeant-major Thomkins, single-handedly resists the Marconicars gang and gradually enlists support from frightened
people.

Although *Dead Cert* is by no means Francis's best novel,
it is a competent thriller and is also important in establishing
many of the techniques and underlying themes that he was to
develop to a high degree in later works. It also demonstrated
from the beginning that he was prepared to pay scrupulous attention to the smallest walk-on character parts, both to secure
credibility and to make points. He is inclined to claim that
much of this is contrived in order "to fill up the book,"[11] but
this is unduly modest and overlooks the fact that he has many
pertinent messages to communicate through the mouths of
his minor characters as a sideline to the main plot. When, for
example, Alan York watches the Marconicars office from a café
he is offended by the illuminated and garish signs desecrating
the building:

> The total effect was colourful indeed, but hardly what
> the Regency architect had had in mind. I had a mental
> picture of him turning in his grave so often that he made
> knots in his winding sheet, and I suppose I smiled, for a
> voice suddenly said, "Vandalism, isn't it?"[12]

The speaker is a middle-aged lady, unidentified by name, who tells Alan that she is associated with an architectural preservation group and makes no secret of her frustration:

> "People just don't seem to care as they should. Would you believe it, half the people in Brighton don't know what a Regency house looks like, when they're surrounded by them all the time?"[13]

Admittedly the lady displays an excessive zeal in buttonholing Alan, which he finds counter-productive, but a point is made nonetheless. There are many small touches like this throughout Francis's novels; he clearly appreciates and understands the old values.

From this point the plot takes an increasingly violent turn, moving sharply toward an exciting climax. At Bristol races the criminals strike back by repeating the trip-wire trick on Alan's horse. The brevity of his hospitalization is evidence of the physical resilience of the Dick Francis heroes, an aspect of his books that has often been unfairly criticized. In this case Alan's injuries serve to bring his father to his bedside from Africa, creating a deeper understanding between them and giving Alan renewed strength to finish the task he has set himself.

Violence again erupts with the brutal murder of the crooked jockey Joe Nantwich, discovered by Alan in circumstances graphically described by Francis, with even a final indication of Joe's petulant nature:

> The scarlet blood suddenly spilled in a gush from his nostrils and welled up in a sticky, bottomless pool in his open mouth. He gave a single choking sound that was almost indecently faint, and over his immature face spread a look of profound astonishment. Then his flesh blanched and his eyes rolled up, and Joe was gone. For several sec-

onds after he died his expression said clearly, "It's not fair." The skin settled in this crisis into the lines most accustomed to it in life.[14]

Alan forces the case to a climax by playing a highly dangerous game, letting it be thought that Joe Nantwich spoke to him before dying. At the racecourse next day, two men attempt to corner Alan but he escapes on horseback. There follows a tremendous chase across country, which maintains a dramatic pace; it typifies the spirit of so much of Francis's work, with Alan the symbol of a lone man on a superb horse and the combined forces of Marconicars pursuing him.

Throughout some ten pages of taut narrative, Francis presents a brilliantly contrived battle between the hunters and the hunted. The ruthless enemy, motorized and armed with guns, proves no match for the intelligence and flexibility of horse and rider in open country. It is an impressive part of the book, which has since become an anthologized classic of equestrian fiction in its own right.

The identity of the boss, the person behind Marconicars and the race fixing, is not difficult to spot fairly early in the story. Francis does not specially favor the whodunit element, preferring usually to identify his villains for what they are and maintaining the reader's interest in other ways. It would be nonetheless questionable to reveal many of the details and the conclusion of *Dead Cert* here, since the Marconicars boss is not the only evildoer to be exposed in the final pages.

With *Dead Cert* Dick Francis immediately showed that he had promise as a writer of thrillers. But would it prove to be a flash in the pan, a singleton of pleasantly surprising distinction? It can now be seen that any doubts of this nature were entirely misplaced. *Nerve* appeared in 1964, closely followed by *For Kicks*, and they showed Francis's developing style and confidence. While dominated by the racing background, they are by no means reruns of his first novel. His

plotting skill and his introduction of entirely new themes—
with *Nerve* a conflict between two men engaged in a psychological war, and *For Kicks* a sort of undercover spy story—
positively belie any suggestion that his specialized background necessitated working to a set formula.

On its publication in New York, *Nerve* was greeted with
enthusiasm by such eminent figures in the crime fiction world
as Stanley Ellin and Ross Macdonald. Their own incisive work
in the field was such that they would not have bestowed
praise without discernment. Similarly Anthony Boucher's
pleasurable surprise has often been subsequently quoted:
"One's reaction is not 'how can a great jockey write such a
good novel?' but rather 'how can such an excellent novelist
know so much about steeplechasing?'"[15]

Nerve opens, as do most of Francis's novels, with a bang.
This time it is literally so, presenting a compulsive invitation
to read on:

> Art Mathews shot himself, loudly and messily, in the
> center of the parade ring at Dunstable races.
> I was standing only six feet away from him, but he did
> it so quickly that had it been only six inches I would not
> have had time to stop him.[16]

The narrator, jockey Rob Finn, observes and analyzes
the reactions of those around him to this totally inexplicable
act. Rob was not a close friend of the dead jockey, and is
aware of only one possible cause for his suicide. Corin Kellar,
a trainer, has been treating Art badly and his constant pressure might just have driven Art to the breaking point. In the
weighing room we meet several other jockeys, their personalities deftly painted by Francis, and their attitudes to the tragedy ranging from sympathy to nonchalance. Most surprising
is the humorless venom of Grant Oldfield, who in recent
months has displayed an unwelcome change of temperament;
having lost his job with top trainer James Axminster, he has

descended into bitterness and aggression and left his former friends wondering about the root cause. Oldfield is a broken man, a fact made clear by Francis with few words and a skillful metaphor:

> Once or twice in the six weeks since the new season had begun I had found him standing with his head thrust forward looking round him in bewilderment, like a bull played out by a matador. A bull exhausted by fighting a piece of cloth, a bull baffled and broken, all his magnificent strength wasted on something he could not pin down with his horns.[17]

At this early stage it does not occur to Rob that a pattern is emerging, that some force is at work insidiously destroying the morale and the reputations of various jockeys, but the reader cannot fail to be intrigued by the changes that have overcome Art Mathews and Grant Oldfield. Rob concentrates his attention upon the suicide of Art Mathews and holds Corin Kellar responsible, but the members of the racing Establishment are not convinced. In particular Ballerton, a pompous steward, would clearly prefer that no doubt be cast upon the behavior of a respected trainer; very aware of his social position and inclined to close ranks, Ballerton is portrayed as a man who relegates jockeys to the lower orders. Rob's opinion on the matter is regarded by Ballerton as insolent and irresponsible mischief.

The suspense in *Nerve* is slow to build up, but the book is no less readable for that. In addition to sharing in Rob's ruminations about the cases of Mathews and Oldfield, and his gradual suspicion that something must have occurred to bring about their rejection by their respective trainers, the reader is again the recipient of Francis's experience as he educates and entertains with many details of racing life. As in *Dead Cert*, he presents a fascinating picture of activity behind the scenes at a racecourse, right down to the minutiae of valets sorting dirty clothes. With Francis one sees more than the glamorous side of the sport. Overshadowing everything is an air of indefinable menace, an atmosphere more significant than the specific question of Art Mathews's death:

> I could see only the symptoms, and see them all the more clearly perhaps since I had been only two years in the game. Between trainers and jockeys there seemed to be an all-round edginess, sudden outbursts of rancor, and an ebbing and flowing undercurrent of resentment and distrust. There was more to it, I thought, than the usual jungle beneath the surface of any fiercely competitive business, more to it than the equivalent of gray-flannel-suit maneuvring in the world of jodhpurs and hacking jackets.[18]

Francis is always anxious to dispel misapprehensions about the social origins, intelligence, and cultural sensitivity of the typical jockey, and indeed to demonstrate that the typical jockey does not exist. In *Dead Cert* he pokes gentle fun at the snobbery of Aunt Deb toward Alan York, and in *Nerve* he takes further steps to demolish the "brawn without brains" falsehood. His jockeys often have impeccable family backgrounds, sometimes from which they are trying to escape, but they also display an educated appreciation of the finer things in life. Here we find Rob Finn living in a Kensington flat with his parents, uncle, and various visiting relatives, all of whom are classical musicians. While Rob does not share their talent and his interest in music is minimal, Francis has established that he comes from a cultured and intellectual family. The fact that he has grown away from them, because of what they see as a break in their musical tradition, is the explanation for his passionate desire to succeed in what he has chosen to do for himself. His parents, in order to be free to pursue their own careers, shuffled him off during childhood to a succession of farm holidays, with the result that he has developed his skill and interest in riding. The disapproval of his family, combined with the knowledge that he is a failure in their eyes, provides Rob with a powerful incentive to build a strong reputation in racing. It later transpires that this theme—failure in one sphere leading to success in another—is to dominate the plot.

The relationships in the Kensington flat are based on mutual coexistence and mere toleration. Rob's family life is negative rather than unhappy, and he is resigned to accept that he is misunderstood to the point where normal daily communication is itself a chore. When he tries to encourage a spark of animated interest by telling his family that a jockey shot himself at the races, the only reaction is his uncle's perplexed "Well, if you will go in for these peculiar pursuits. . . ."

Rob's contacts with the opposite sex provide little consolation. His girlfriend, a model called Paulina, is still on affectionate terms with him but has decided on marital security with a middle-aged aristocratic tycoon. Rob is in any case more intent upon a future with his attractive cousin Joanna, a singer in the Finn family tradition, but again this relationship has caused him great torment:

> I had several times asked her to marry me, but she always said no. First cousins, she explained firmly, were too closely related. Besides which, she added, I didn't stir her blood.[19]

The emotions of Rob, seemingly destined to a platonic love but wanting much more, are well conveyed. When Joanna first appears, her role is that of the only member of the family with whom Rob can have an intelligent and open conversation. As the book progresses and they are drawn closely together by events, Francis explores with feeling the doubts and fears felt by Joanna, her love for Rob overshadowed and frustrated by an unshakable belief that a sexual relationship between them would be wrong.

The pivotal character of *Nerve*, however, proves to be

the personable and charismatic television personality Maurice Kemp-Lore. Racing commentator and host of a weekly chat show, he is held in awe by jockeys, trainers, and owners and wields considerable influence. At an early point the reader is told that his father is a mainstay of the National Hunt Committee and once rode a Grand National winner, while his sister is a champion of equestrian events. His own asthmatic allergy to horses has resulted in his failure to live up to his family's skills in horsemanship, but this has motivated him to excel in his chosen career and he has become the ultimate in charming and confident media figures. One can detect the similarity between Kemp-Lore and Rob Finn, both men driven by their inability to toe the customary family line, but Rob comes to suspect that much more lurks beneath the Kemp-Lore story.

The demoralization and disgrace of various jockeys continues to occur. The latest victim is the impecunious young Peter Cloony, who is prevented by accidents from arriving on time for his rides and rapidly develops a reputation for unreliability. In contrast Rob himself begins to achieve considerable success on James Axminster's horses, displacing the regular jockey Grant Oldfield and being physically attacked by Oldfield in return. When Rob begins to think again of the desperation, the mental disturbance, and the unemployment that has overcome the jockeys, he suspects that a pattern exists but it does not occur to him that soon he will be fighting the mysterious force himself. At this stage, by carefully using a succession of incidents and some subtle insinuation, Francis has planted in the mind of the reader the idea of a systematic campaign to ruin the jockeys. There is too much coincidence: it *has* to be planned. The accidents, the rumors of dishonesty and fecklessness, the suggestions of poor performance, are being fed to owners and trainers by calculated use of the "grapevine" so that the source of such stories is difficult to trace.

The possibility that Maurice Kemp-Lore is orchestrating this campaign of hate occurs to the reader, if not so swiftly to Rob Finn. The maliciousness of Kemp-Lore, while sheltering behind a façade of manufactured bonhomie, is evident when he invites Rob to appear on his live television program. He creates a conflict between Rob and his other guest, the bullying steward John Ballerton, but is careful to keep his own position of impartial chairman and to preserve his public image. With facile skill Kemp-Lore maneuvers the two men into a confrontation, knowing it will be simple to extract from the bigoted Ballerton a harsh comment about unsuccessful and low-paid jockeys. Kemp-Lore's carefully staged controversy fizzles out when Rob redeems the situation with a heartfelt defense:

> I spoke truthfully, vehemently, and straight from the heart, "Give me a horse and a race to ride it in, and I don't care if I wear silks or . . . or . . . pajamas. I don't care if there's anyone watching or not. I don't care if I don't earn much money, or if I break my bones, or if I have to starve to keep my weight down. All I care about is racing . . . racing . . . and winning, if I can."[20]

It is nonetheless obvious to Rob that he was not intended to emerge from the program as a winner and he feels a strange apprehensiveness.

There is little opportunity for Rob to muse further about the complex character and motives of Kemp-Lore at this point, as shortly afterwards he begins to enjoy outstanding success on James Axminster's horses. He is nevertheless reminded of the matter when Axminster remarks upon the current shortage of good jockeys, adding that whenever he finds an up-and-coming prospect he seems to hear something to the jockey's disadvantage.

The hoodoo at first appears to be something from which Rob has been blessedly free. Then suddenly he begins to lose races. Of seventeen horses, fifteen finish in the rear of the field, and Rob is unable to understand all but two of the results. Within a short period of time, Rob is pitched from the pinnacle of success to the depths of disgrace. He is greeted with embarrassed silence by some friends, open contempt by others, while a minority of them display sympathy bordering upon pity. Gossip is rife, and James Axminster is the first to put it to Rob: the word is out, he says, that Rob has lost his nerve and now always keeps in the background out of trouble.

Rob is utterly alone in his conviction that there is a mystery surrounding what has happened to him. He knows that he has not lost his nerve, and that any change has taken place in the horses rather than in himself, yet all witnesses including the gloating Ballerton have the evidence of their own eyes. Francis paints a stark picture of a man in isolation, the victim of whispers and open derision, aware of his innocence but with no trace of explanation. Rob clings desperately to his last chance, the possibility of winning the important Midwinter Gold Cup. Press reports are against him, while Kemp-Lore is insidiously provoking comments about him from his television guests. Rob's descent is such that he almost loses belief in himself.

Francis takes us through Rob's thought processes, showing that only with extreme difficulty can he manage to take a grip on himself, to control his destiny. He is still his own man, rather than the wreck created by his misfortune. Psychiatric advice convinces him that his suspicions of Kemp-Lore could be well founded, and that the man's motivation begins as a parallel to Rob's own but is then distorted into obsessive hatred:

> "If this were a hypothetical case I would tell you that such a man could both hate and envy his father—and his sister—and have felt both these emotions from early childhood. But because he knows these feelings are wrong he represses them, and the aggression is unfortu-

nately transferred onto people who show the same qualities and abilities that he hates in his father. Such individuals can be helped. They can be understood and treated,
and forgiven."
    "I can't forgive him," I said. "And I'm going to stop
him."[21]

The key point in *Nerve*, indeed the point that occurs in
all of Francis's books, has thus been reached. The hero, to
protect himself and in retaliation for what has befallen others,
is about to turn against the aggressor and to show unexpected
vehemence in the process. While Kemp-Lore's rumors are
not criminal, he is directly responsible for Art Mathews's suicide. Assuming that he is guilty of doping Rob's horses to ensure their poor performance, his behavior has moved from
mental aberration to a willingness to break the law. All this
makes it essential for Rob to prove him guilty to his own satisfaction, and to secure his own poetic justice rather than the
gentlemanly, old-school-tie justice of the National Hunt Committee.

How Rob carries this through, in the process being
subjected to excruciating physical torture by his adversary, makes for uncomfortable but compulsive reading. Francis presents not only a perceptive study of Rob, his inner
strengths and his physical resilience both responding positively to enormous pressure, but he also shows how far Kemp-
Lore is willing to go in inflicting degradation upon fellow-
beings as he gradually loses his mind.

In addition to being a suspenseful story on an unusual
noncriminal theme that builds to a well-rounded and just conclusion, *Nerve* touches upon three interesting areas. First, it
raises questions about the border line between madness and
criminality. Second, there is the incestuous label that Joanna
attaches to a marriage between first cousins, a debate that
Francis does not neatly tie up; although it appears that a per-
manent relationship might develop between Rob and Joanna,
the reader is left uncertain of this.

Third, there is the theme that relates directly to the reader in identifying with Rob's dilemma. How does one feel when all friends and colleagues believe something that one knows to be untrue, but that defies all attempts to disprove? How much worse would one feel if this accusation strikes at the very roots of one's day-to-day existence? Loss of nerve is the ultimate destruction of a chase jockey, but what if this happened to the reader? Francis impels one to ask what is required of oneself in order to preserve sanity and maintain self-respect, by showing what qualities Rob Finn has to call upon if he is to swing the balance back in his favor.

There is little similarity between *Nerve* and *Dead Cert*, save the qualities of the central character. In one step only, from an absorbing tale of crime to a book that is no less a thriller but is principally an examination of the evil that stems from one man's distorted mentality, Francis displayed a versatility and intelligence giving ample indication that he could become a writer of some consequence, rather than a hack producing a series of dull variations on a restrictive theme. Even his third novel *For Kicks*, while concentrating upon criminal conspiracy in the world of racing, had much about it that was fresh and new and was as thought-provoking as its predecessors.

The central character of *For Kicks*, Daniel Roke, owns a prosperous stud farm in Australia. He is visited by the Earl of October, a member of the National Hunt Committee in England, with a request to return to the old country to investigate a horse-doping racket as an undercover agent. All that is known is that ten unlikely winners have apparently been stimulated in some way, but tests have all proved negative. In addition, an investigative racing journalist has been killed in a car crash.

Daniel is reluctant, but Francis shows the factors between which he is torn. His original intention to take up the law, in the footsteps of his father, was thwarted by the death of his parents, leaving him to care for two sisters and a

brother. In spite of the success of the stud farm he established, it holds little excitement for him. "There lay my
prison," he muses, sitting on a high rock surveying his property and meditating upon October's tempting offer. Obviously his reluctance can be overcome, his surface resistance
being eroded by the frustration of a life that is strangely
empty. There is no doubt of the strength of his love for the
family, but "the feeling that I had built a prosperous trap for
myself had slowly eaten away the earlier contentment I had
found in providing for them."[22] It is possible to envy Daniel's
prosperity, yet understand his longing:

> To have something else to remember but the proces-
> sion of profitable days, something else to see besides the
> beauty with which I was surrounded. I had been so busy
> stuffing worms down my fellow nestlings' throats that I
> had never stretched my wings.[23]

The first problem for Daniel, having flown to England, is
where and how to start his inquiries. October employs him as
a stable lad in his Yorkshire establishment, where the disreputable appearance and shady character he has contrived soon
make him a talking point. October's manager, Inskip, is
treated reverentially by the other lads but Daniel's acquaintance with what he recognizes as "the almost aggressive egali-
tarianism of Australia" makes it scarcely necessary for him to
act the role of the rebel. There is in his character a rejection of
those who treat subordinates as inferiors, and he regards pas-
sive acceptance of authority as undignified and shameful.
Francis is accomplished in building up the picture of his protagonist by showing his beliefs and the influences that have
given rise to them.

Romantic interest, rarely a significant strand in Francis's
books, is particularly slight in *For Kicks*. Admittedly there are
the almost obligatory attractive girls, in this case the daugh-
ters of Lord October, one of whom is sexually provocative and

traps Daniel in a compromising situation that results in his dismissal. October feels he has a duty to believe his daughter's story rather than Daniel's, but in the event the dismissal serves a useful purpose. The stage has been reached when Daniel's unreliability and apparent lack of trustworthiness has come to the attention of men from the disreputable stables that Daniel suspects might be connected with the doping.

Careful study of all the suspect cases has indicated that the horses had all won "selling chases," races where the winner is subsequently auctioned, and that two men called Hedley Humber and Paul James Adams had either owned or trained nine of the horses concerned at some stage in their racing careers. Humber owns stables at which no responsible lads wish to work or at least to remain for long, and it is Humber's establishment to which Daniel turns in search of a job. A neat touch—a fond farewell to the good things in life before delivering himself up to Humber's tender mercies—sees Daniel (still looking villainous in person and in dress) at a smart hotel incongruously consuming lobster, duck bigarade, lemon soufflé, brie, and a bottle of Chateau Leauville Lescases 1948. This is another sly dig on Francis's part, consciously or unconsciously pointing out that his sometimes rough-and-ready characters are not uncultured or ignorant of the world's more sophisticated pleasures.

The discomforting and degrading regime of Hedley Humber's stables quickly becomes apparent. The tyrannical Humber himself, by a combination of overworking his lads and beating them into submission when the fancy takes him, ensures quite deliberately that the turnover rate of his employees is high. A job with Humber is the last resort of any stable lad who is physically or emotionally inadequate, or whose character and record leave much to be desired, so the loss of that job means leaving racing altogether and taking Humber's secrets away with them. While they are given little opportunity to learn of his shady activities, what they do learn is thus neatly kept from the more respectable racing fraternity. All in all, the atmosphere of Humber's establishment is painfully reminiscent of that at Dotheboys Hall, where Dickens's Nicholas Nickleby rebels against the vicious Wackford Squeers and befriends the cringing Smike (in this case the retarded youth Jerry).

Working undercover, Daniel sets out to unearth Humber's involvement with the horse doping. Much self-analysis becomes necessary on his part, since the retention of his cover permits no relaxation in his efforts to appear slovenly in dress and performance, uncouth in manner, and crafty in nature.

> If one pretended long enough to be a wreck, did one finally become one? I wondered. And if one stripped oneself continuously of all human dignity, would one in the end be unaware of its absence?[24]

This is an interesting point, and one not merely academic; Daniel has to strive conscientiously to ensure that pretense does not become reality.

In time it is clear that Hedley Humber, together with his associate Paul James Adams, are the men behind the racket. Since the horses must be treated in some way while in the possession of Humber or Adams—long before they unexpectedly win crucial races—the use of dope is out of the question. The mystery element of *For Kicks* is basically the puzzle of how the fixing of horses is achieved by the villains. It is not a whodunit, since the characters of Humber and Adams are made crystal clear; the reader is presented with complete pictures of evil and sadistic rogues, and is in no doubt as to their guilt.

In this milieu of violence and ruthlessness, Francis relieves the tension by injecting a touch of compassion and reaches our feelings with the relationship between Daniel and

the mentally subnormal stable lad Jerry. Daniel befriends the
unfortunate Jerry, becoming an older brother or father figure,
taking him for outings to town and reading his comics aloud to
him. His reward is Jerry's pathetic devotion. This is far removed from the perceived world of racing, the glamour and
the physical prowess, and is a revealing example of how
Francis strives to introduce the human factor, the delicate
personal touches. He does it superbly, extending Daniel's
feelings for Jerry beyond a superficial and sentimental attach-
ment:

> He fetched the comic from the cardboard box in which
> he kept his few belongings and sat beside me while I read
> him the captions. . . . We went through the whole thing
> at least twice, with him laughing contentedly and repeat-
> ing the words after me. By the end of the week he would
> know most of them by heart.

As Daniel watches Jerry, he tries to imagine the thinking process of a brain "like cotton wool" that has no awareness of the
world as it really is, and he ruefully reflects that life on that
level has its compensations:

> If one didn't realize one was an object of calculated hu-
> miliations, there would be no need to try to make oneself
> be insensitive to them. If I had his simplicity, I thought,
> I would find life at Humber's very much easier.
> He looked up suddenly and saw me watching him, and
> gave me a warm, contented, trusting smile.
> "I like you," he said; and turned his attention back to
> the paper.[25]

During Daniel's turbulent employment with Humber,
an interlude occurs that is to develop into a frightening complication. He is invited by October's elder daughter Lady
Elinor, a student at Durham University, to visit her. He does
so, still in his disreputable clothes and bearing his increasingly automatic air of surliness, but the university has a stabil-

izing and telling effect on him as he observes with envy that
his parents' death has robbed him of the time and opportunity
to study in such civilized surroundings.

Elinor has discovered from her younger sister the truth
about the alleged sexual assault by Daniel, and now knows
that her father's reaction was unjust. She now begins to see
Daniel in his true light, her conversation with him providing
various indications that he is a cultured and sympathetic man
rather than an oafish and surly illiterate. Yet Daniel is not free
to explain to her the reason for his deception, and Elinor is
left puzzled by the masquerade and his many contradictions.
Later she is unwittingly responsible for blowing Daniel's
cover to Humber and Adams, with horrifyingly violent results.

The villains' means of manipulating the horses will not be
revealed here. Suffice it to say that it is a technique of un-
speakable cruelty. One prefers always to think of Francis's
plots as authentic, stemming from his own vast experience in
the racing world; the activities of Humber and Adams, while
scientifically plausible, are so extreme that one retains the belief that such monsters do not exist in the real world. They are
much larger than life, but Francis's narrative power and characterization is such that they must be despised rather than
dismissed.

Daniel Roke is a loner. In spite of physical discomfort
and the very real possibility of following his predecessor the
investigative reporter into oblivion, he realizes that working
as an undercover agent has filled a gap in his previously well-
ordered and prosperous existence. On being asked by Lord
October why he agreed to do it, he replies, "For kicks, I sup-
pose." Rather than yearn to go back to his family and business
in Australia, and to regard October's assignment as an exciting and dangerous interlude, he now has a calling that he
finds impossible to resist. "Very few novels," said Anthony
Boucher, "have done a comparably penetrating job of study-

ing the effect of detection upon the character of the detective himself."[26]

For Kicks began to consolidate the impression made upon the reading public by *Dead Cert* and *Nerve*, that of a highly promising and versatile novelist in the field of suspense. In its own right it is a good crime story, hence the award of the Silver Dagger by the Crime Writers' Association in the United Kingdom, but Francis was capable of an even higher standard later recognized by no less an authority than C. P. Snow: "In a book such as *For Kicks* the suspense, the plot ingenuity, the underlying authority are all there, but the verbal sharpness and the psychological riches are still to come."[27]

3

The Hero as Halley

Odds Against
Whip Hand

Odds Against saw the introduction of Francis's only series character. The term is really a misnomer, since Sid Halley only reappeared in *Whip Hand* fourteen years later but was also the hero of a series of original television scripts called *The Racing Game*. It is appropriate to deal here with *Whip Hand* out of chronological sequence, with the added interest that a long period separated the two books and Francis thus presented himself with the opportunity to reassess one of his most intriguing character creations.

When the reader first meets Sid Halley in *Odds Against*, he is in a hospital bed. Employed by the Radnor Detective Agency as a courtesy to his influential father-in-law, Sid has been shot while investigating a case of intimidation. His physical resilience is in no doubt; as his boss Radnor tells the doctor, his body has already had to endure multiple fractures and injuries sustained during a career as a steeplechase jockey. This is the career for which Sid still has a passionate yearning,

37

his outstanding success having been terminated by an accident that left him with a severely damaged hand. Sid's colleagues at the detective agency view his deformity with embarrassment and never mention it, the sole exception being his friend Chico Barnes, a happy-go-lucky youngster for whom diplomacy has little meaning.

Radnor's agency is large and reputable, with a specialist section that deals in racing matters. Sid is painfully aware that his acceptance by Radnor is an act of pity and that his father-in-law has pulled strings, but at first he cares little. Self-respect and confidence are at a low ebb since the fateful accident, and his boredom and emptiness of spirit have been aggravated by three years of separation from his wife Jenny.

Chico Barnes is in some respects on a par with Sid, but in his case insecurity manifests itself as an aggressive liveliness, an arrogant carelessness of manner. At twenty-four, he has suffered the life of a disadvantaged child since being abandoned in infancy. He could easily have taken the path to delinquency, but instead has used his quickness of mind and body to good effect in his work for Radnor, his sometimes unconventional skills at judo and wrestling making him a useful operative and a perfect complement to Sid Halley.

Sid's father-in-law, retired Rear Admiral Charles Roland, has maintained contact with Sid since the separation. This is in itself surprising, since Roland opposed the marriage, but their mutual interest in chess and Roland's developing enthusiasm for racing have bred mutual respect and understanding. One of the factors finally binding them together is that Roland has become a steward at several racecourses.

Following his discharge from the hospital, Sid visits Roland's country home at Aynsford and finds him unpacking specimens of quartz borrowed from an institute of mineralogy. From Roland's cryptic remarks it appears that they are intended as bait to attract his weekend guests, the van Dysarts and the Krayes. Sid spends little time pondering this; he is far more concerned about the radio news that Seabury racecourse has been damaged by spillage as a result of a tanker accident. Some months earlier, Sid knows, racing at Seabury was similarly interrupted by a stable fire and again by the collapse of some surface drainage. Sid's thoughts are sentimental rather than suspicious, as he has raced many times at Seabury and the news story has reactivated the ache he feels for his lost life.

Sid takes an instant and wholly justified dislike to Roland's guests. The van Dysarts and the Krayes treat him with contempt, which is menacingly encouraged by Roland himself. At the dinner table, Roland refers derisively to Sid's illegitimacy, his working-class background, his diminutive size, his crippled hand, and his lack of education. Suffering this humiliating onslaught in silence, Sid can only assume that Roland's attitude towards him is a bullying stance he has adopted for the benefit of his guests. Roland later explains his plan: to obtain their confidence by posing as a collector of quartz, while destroying Sid in their eyes and revealing him to be of little consequence as an opponent.

The principal object of Roland's attention is Howard Kraye, whom he suspects of engineering the downfall of Seabury racecourse and acquiring control of its shares. Kraye's ultimate intention, Roland believes, is to sell the course for redevelopment. Roland is out to stop him with Sid's help.

During the weekend, while the Krayes play cat and mouse with Sid, Francis inserts a simple interlude that tells something of Sid and his emotions and fills in the background of his broken marriage. In it, Sid takes a tender look around his wife Jenny's room, still with its girlish furnishings and old toys, and reflects upon their relationship and how it disintegrated. His own ambition and the discipline of his work as a

jockey conflicted with Jenny's ideal lifestyle, and Sid was
forced to choose between them. Now he wonders if he chose
wisely:

> It was just life's little irony that six months later I lost the
> racing as well. Gradually since then I had come to realize
> that a marriage didn't break up just because one half liked
> parties and the other didn't. I thought now that Jenny's
> insistence on a gay time was the result of my having failed
> her in some basic, deeply necessary way. Which did
> nothing whatsoever for my self-respect or my self-confi-
> dence.[1]

So far the reader has not met Jenny herself, and sympathy for Sid raises prejudices against her. Nevertheless there is
the impression that Sid is a difficult man to live with, and the
reader reserves judgment.

No such reservations can apply to Howard and Doria
Kraye, who are among the most odious and vicious characters
created by Francis. Their contemptuous taunting of Sid is evil
enough, as they play with him in a manner they erroneously
feel will ingratiate them with Charles Roland, but shortly afterwards they extend this to physical abuse in a scene that
ranks high among those occasioning charges of sadism against
Francis. The Krayes forcibly expose his crippled hand and in-
flict pain on him, merely because Sid is judged to have in-
sulted Doria Kraye.

> They looked steadily at the wasted, flabby, twisted hand,
> and at the scars on my forearm, wrist and palm, not only
> the terrible jagged marks of the original injury but the
> several tidier ones of the operations I had had since. It
> was a mess, a right and proper mess. . . .
>   He stiffened his free hand and chopped the edge of it
> across the worst part, the inside of my wrist. I jerked in
> his grasp.[2]

Sadism? As ever, this depends upon the context. Here
the actions amply demonstrate the callous nature of those
with whom Sid is dealing, and are completely in character.

Gratuitous violence is clearly the norm for Howard Kraye, and this in itself fires Sid with the will to investigate their activities further, to give new life to the sinecure role he has hitherto played at the Radnor agency and which has suddenly become inadequate. To Radnor, who is persuaded to take up the affair of Seabury racecourse on behalf of the stewards, the change in Sid is so marked that he likens it to the awakening of a zombie.

Kraye's violence motivates Sid to hit back, and to prove that Kraye is responsible for the "accidents" destroying Seabury as an economic proposition for racing purposes. A further incentive is Sid's love of racing and his passion to preserve good courses. This is dear to the heart of Dick Francis himself, who has sadly witnessed the demise of several racecourses due to the unrestrained pursuit of financial gain in the property market. It was the fate of the Hurst Park course that gave him the basic idea for *Odds Against*,[3] and it must also have encouraged him to put some emotional words in the mouth of Sid Halley:

> Chasing owners, I thought, should rise up in a body and demand that Seabury should be preserved, because no racecourse was better for their horses. But of course they wouldn't. You could tell owners how good it was, but unless they were horsemen themselves, it didn't register. They only saw the rotten amenities of the stands, not the splendidly sited well-built fences that positively invited their horses to jump. They didn't know how their horses relished the short springy turf underfoot, or found the arc and cambers of the bends perfect for maintaining an even speed. . . .[4]

Sid poses as an investor in order to make contact with Kraye's stockbroker Ellis Bolt, and it is at Bolt's office that he meets his receptionist Zanna Martin. At the time of his visit she is preparing letters from a list of Seabury shareholders, but Sid's intention to meet her again outside the office is prompted only partly by her potential as an informant. He is

also intrigued by the fact that her desk is deliberately placed
in an inconspicuous position, and that she seems reluctant to
face him. On closer inspection he sees the reason: scars on her
face and a false eye that he later learns were the result of a fire-
works accident. Sadly he reflects that the scars are old but the
inner wound has never healed—a condition he knows only
too well. In his own case his whole attitude of mind has been
affected, and on another occasion Sid concisely defines his
feelings while watching travelers at an airport:

> So much expectation in the faces, as if they could fly away
> and leave their troubles on the ground. An illusion, I
> thought sourly. Your troubles flew with you; a drag in the
> mind . . . a deformity in the pocket.[5]

When Sid and Zanna meet again, their conversation is as
much about their injuries and their effects upon them as
about the affairs of Ellis Bolt and Howard Kraye. With determination Sid takes the unusual step of removing his crippled
hand from his pocket for Zanna to see, and they strike a
bargain—Zanna is to reposition her desk so as to face all call-
ers, and Sid is to leave his hand on view outside his pocket.
Neither, however, is confident of keeping faith with the
other. Yet there is a developing relationship between these
two people, their lives cruelly affected by comparatively minor tragedies that produced repercussions out of all proportion. Sid's career has been ruined, while Zanna is afraid to
look into a mirror, and both have been taking pitifully obvious
steps to hide their deformities from observation. Francis
creates a picture of two characters who are both inherently
strong, but whose traces of self-pity can only be conquered by
mutual support.

Charles Roland believes that Sid cares little about the ca-
lamities in his life, whether it is Jenny's wish for a divorce or
his injury that halted a career Sid once described as a good

run for his money. In reality Sid's nonchalance is false, a manifestation of his rejection of sympathy that goes back much further in time, from his illegitimacy and through his poverty-striken childhood.

One of the many crises Sid must overcome occurs at the moment when Zanna discovers his true reason for visiting Bolt's office and cultivating her acquaintance. He is then faced with her feeling that she has been used, and that the public exposure of her deformity was all a cruel game. It requires understanding, and a strength of character Sid does not know he possesses, to persuade her to accept his sincerity. Francis approaches the relationship with careful thought, and shows two human beings jointly working out the problems that they previously felt insoluble. It matters little that they are man and woman. Sex does not enter into it. In Zanna's case there is only a developing trust in Sid, and a gradual transformation.

When Sid is finally cornered by the racketeers, there are further scenes of violence and another stark passage where his injured hand is again the victim of torture:

> He hit my wrist with the poker. I'd hoped he might at least try to be subtle, but instead he used all his strength and with that one first blow smashed the whole shooting match to smithereens. The poker broke through the skin. The bones cracked audibly like sticks. . . .
> He put the tip of the poker on my shattered bleeding wrist and gave a violent jerk. Among other things it felt like a fizzing electric shock, up my arm into my head and down to my toes.[6]

It is straightforward, clear and convincing. Again it is consistent with the vicious character of Howard Kraye, whose twin objectives are inflicting pain and extracting information. While one must agree with John C. Carr that this scene depicts violence that goes "past the gag level,"[7] the sadism is

Howard Kraye's rather than Francis's. There is a need for Francis to convey this without sparing the details, and the reader understands Sid's thoughts as he suffers:

> I thought about the people who had borne the beatings and brutalities of the Nazis and of the Japanese and had often died without betraying their secrets. I thought about the atrocities still going on throughout the world, and the ease with which man could break man. . . .
> Too young for World War Two, safe in a tolerant society, I had had no thought that I should ever come to such a test. To suffer or to talk. The dilemma that stretched back to antiquity.[8]

Following the exciting climax of *Odds Against*, good comes from evil when Sid is introduced to the possibilities of a myoelectric hand. The attention paid by Kraye to his deformed hand was so severe that it had to be amputated. Although Sid can look forward to the benefits of a new hand brought about by modern technology, he will still experience uncertainties and traumas that might never completely disappear:

> My unconscious mind did its best to reject the facts: I dreamed each night that I was whole, riding races, tying knots, clapping—anything which required two hands. I awoke to the frustrating stump.[9]

At this point *Odds Against* is concluded, and no one in 1965 can have expected that the story of Sid Halley would be resumed. It was not until the late 1970s, by which time Dick Francis the writer had been firmly established as a household name in the United Kingdom, that Sid reemerged. Yorkshire Television filmed a series of six Halley adventures under the collective title *The Racing Game*, adapting *Odds Against* as the first and using five entirely new stories; Francis did not write the scripts, but acted as technical adviser and provided the story lines. They were shown in the United Kingdom in 1979, and in the United States (in the series *Mystery!*) in 1980 and 1981. The making of these television movies prompted Francis to break his tradition and write a new novel featuring his earlier hero.

Mike Gwilym, the Royal Shakespeare Company actor who so brilliantly played Sid Halley in the television series, inspired Francis to write *Whip Hand*. A fellow Welshman, Gwilym became a close friend of Dick and Mary Francis. "Whenever I met him," says Francis, "I knew that this *was* Sid Halley and I began to ask myself what had happened to Sid after *Odds Against*. I had to find out."[10] At the end of *Odds Against* Sid Halley no longer has a deformed hand: he has lost it completely. "In *Whip Hand*," Francis tells us in his autobiography, "I set out to explore the mental difficulties of someone coming to terms with such a loss. In the event, it proved a most disturbing book to write, a psychological wringer which gave me insomnia for months."[11] The recurrent threat to Sid in *Whip Hand* is that he will lose his other hand if he refuses to cooperate with the villains, and the shattering effect of this possibility upon Sid is bound to have troubled Francis during the writing, when he was constantly visualizing Sid as his own friend Gwilym. There is also no doubt that Francis has a closer affinity with Sid Halley and feels more intensely what Sid feels than any of his other protagonists.

The fact that the series *The Racing Game* inspired his renewed interest in Sid was acknowledged by Francis when he dedicated *Whip Hand* to Mike Gwilym and to Jacky Stoller, the producer of the series, "with gratitude and affection." It was hailed by critics as his best novel for some time, and Francis was seen as at the top of his form. In the United States, with Francis's low profile raised higher by the television series, he achieved really dramatic popular success with *Whip Hand* as the first of his books to appear on the *New York*

Times bestseller list. It was awarded the Gold Dagger by the Crime Writers' Association in the United Kingdom and the Edgar by the Mystery Writers of America, a double distinction that *Whip Hand* shares only with John le Carré's *The Spy Who Came in from the Cold* and John Ball's *In the Heat of the Night*.

Whip Hand opens with a prologue in which Sid Halley dreams of winning a race. He remarked upon such dreams at the conclusion of *Odds Against*, but here it appears in its worst manifestation. In his mind he is still a jockey, experiencing the exhilaration and the will to win, spurred on by the cheering of the crowd. When he wakes, he realizes for the millionth time that he will never race again, and the reader sees that he is beginning to come to terms with his life:

> I dreamed it quite often.
> Damned senseless thing to do.
> Living, of course, was quite different. One discarded dreams, and got dressed, and made what one could of the day.[12]

Although it is not specifically stated, *Whip Hand* appears to take up Sid's story quite shortly after the events narrated in *Odds Against*. He is still becoming accustomed to his myoelectric hand, and his career as a private detective is described as recent. Friends in the racing world are beginning to accept him as successful in his new calling, rather than regarding him as an ex-jockey in limbo.

Sid's new case begins when he is visited by Rosemary Caspar, the wife of an internationally successful trainer whose best horses have unaccountably begun to fail. Thus the reader is immediately faced with a typical Dick Francis mystery— why have the horses suddenly lost their earlier form, why can the vets find no cause, and will the same thing happen to George Caspar's latest champion?

But *Whip Hand* is more than a superlative racing mystery. Further insight is given into Sid's relationships with father-in-law Charles Roland and ex-wife Jenny, crisply summarized as:

> We had been married for five years; two in happiness, two in discord, and one in bitterness; and now only the itching half-mended wounds remained. Those, and the friendship of her father, which I had come by with difficulty and now prized as the only treasure saved from the wreck.[13]

In *Whip Hand* Jenny is in trouble. She has been used as a front by a confidence trickster, and now faces prosecution. This is case number two for Sid, in a book that presents an unusual intermingling of mysteries rather than one straight plot. It is impossible for Sid to separate his own feelings for Jenny from his professional involvement in her current problem; the divorce has been a mere formality that cannot prevent the old love-hate emotions from erupting whenever the two of them meet.

No sooner has Sid agreed to look into Jenny's difficulties than he is approached by racehorse owner Lord Friarly with yet another commission, to investigate the suspected fixing of horses owned by outwardly respectable syndicates. This is quickly followed by a request from Commander Wainwright, the Jockey Club's Director of Security, to carry out an unofficial inquiry to ascertain if his deputy has been taking bribes. Thus Sid's life is very full, and overcommitment on these cases inclines him to seek out his friend Chico Barnes. Chico is now teaching judo and helping Sid occasionally in his one-man detective agency, since the sudden death of Radnor has forced them to go their separate ways.

Jenny has a strange attitude toward Sid's willingness to help her. Although she urgently needs to find Nicholas Ashe, the man who pocketed considerable sums through a fake charity and disappeared leaving her with the responsibility, she seems unable to control her aggressiveness and arrogance. There is nevertheless an occasional sense of deliberately cultivated antipathy, disguising an affection for Sid that has remained as a fragment of their former relationship. To interested spectators she belittles Sid, saying that the task of finding Ashe is beyond his capabilities; then, when he disagrees, she cruelly comments, "It's pathetic how he longs to prove he's clever, now he's disabled."[14] Sid invariably retaliates on such occasions, although not with such venom, this time remarking, "If I find Nicholas Ashe I'll give him to Jenny. Poor fellow."[15]

Jenny met Ashe while on the rebound from her marriage to Sid, and felt that he could offer her something her marriage had lacked. It is specially painful for Jenny to reflect that Ashe's exuberance and fun-loving lifestyle reminded her of the way Sid used to be, and this made the change in Sid even more difficult to bear.

> Perhaps it was too much, even for her. How could people, I wondered for the ten thousandth time, how could people who loved so dearly come to such a wilderness; and yet the change in us was irreversible, and neither of us would even search for a way back. It was impossible. The fire was out. Only a few live coals lurked in the ashes, searing unexpectedly at the incautious touch.[16]

This is writing of high quality, lucid and pertinent, as Francis seeks the indefinable reasons why a loving and stable union can become stale and turn almost to hatred.

By coincidence Jenny is indirectly responsible for bringing a new love into Sid's life. While examining Ashe's papers at her apartment, he meets her live-in friend Louise McInnes who begins to assist him in his inquiries. They find themselves drawn together, and she is a refreshing contrast to Jenny in personality and temperament, genuinely working to understand Sid, his problems and his motivation. Jenny neither understands nor sympathizes with Sid, and makes no attempt to appreciate his appetite for his former or current careers. Even his disablement provokes little compassion from her:

> "If you'd done as I asked, and given up racing, you wouldn't have lost it."
> "Probably not."
> "You'd have a hand, not half an arm . . . not a stump.
> . . . Racing first. Always racing. Dedication and winning and glory. And me nowhere. It serves you right. We'd still have been married . . . you'd still have your hand . . . if you'd have given up your precious racing when I wanted you to. Being champion jockey meant more to you than I did."[17]

Sid's protest, that he was a jockey when they met and she knew what it entailed, is surprisingly weak. The reader senses some justification for Jenny's apparent intolerance, imagining the frustrations of sharing life with a man who is addicted to danger. The fact that Sid is persisting with another perilous career even after his accident, even after the complete destruction of his hand by Howard Kraye, is ample evidence to Jenny that there can be no recipe for a normal married life with him.

There is a streak of maliciousness in Jenny, but credence can still be given to her implication that Sid has been selfish. Dick Francis himself has enjoyed a happy marriage with a partner who understood and participated in his passion for racing and whatever motivates a jockey to continue despite injuries and disappointments. In describing the breakdown of Sid and Jenny's marriage, he presents very fairly the strains that can be inflicted by the sport; recognizing his own good fortune, he tells of the downward path relationships can take in this situation. What is more, leaving aside Jenny's vindictiveness, Francis is evenhanded in his treatment and the reader's sympathies lie not exclusively with Sid.

Sid has to turn from his self-analysis and heart-searching in Jenny's case to the other investigations with which he is concerned. On the question of George Caspar's failing horses, Sid and Chico find that they all appeared to suffer from heart problems. Sid is also fully occupied with the alleged corruption at the Jockey Club, and it becomes clear that the corruption and the suspect syndicates mentioned by Lord Friarly are interrelated. There can also be no doubt of the viciousness of the criminals concerned.

Francis's special skill at building into his stories peaks of suspense at various points, often totally unexpected, can be seen again here. Straightforward (though never dull) passages of narrative, while inquiries are being pursued, suddenly erupt into action and violence. Thus at this juncture, with Sid carefully attempting to piece together his findings about the various cases, he is abducted by the villains concerned with the George Caspar investigation and subjected to a form of mental torture that is calculated to be most effective in his case. A crowbar wielded by one of the villains becomes the symbol of Sid's ultimate fear, that his one good hand will be destroyed, but his principal adversary has something quicker and infinitely more destructive in mind.

A promise is made to Sid that his hand will be demolished by the chief villain's shotgun if he refuses to abandon the Caspar inquiry. It is no hollow threat, and it is totally effective. Sid does precisely as they demand, leaving them free to fix Caspar's latest champion in an important race. No one can understand Sid's sudden withdrawal of interest from the case, and he finds it impossible to reject the contempt in which Rosemary Caspar now holds him. His mental torment, shared by the reader, finally resolves itself into a decision to fight back:

I thought that what I had lost might be worse than a hand. For a hand there were substitutes which could grip and look passable. But if the core of oneself had crumbled, how could one manage at all? . . . I wondered which crippled one worse, amputation without or within.

Humiliation and rejection and helplessness and failure. . . .

After all these years I would *not*, I thought wretchedly, I would damned well *not* be defeated by fear.[18]

Time and again Francis returns to the turmoil of emotions suffered by Sid Halley, the impossible choice between remaining a coward in his own estimation or risking physical mutilation. Sid reflects that his artificial hand has given him comfort and support, the independence of action in day-to-day matters without having to rely upon embarrassed friends to make allowances for his incapacity. With one good hand, he feels, he is self-sufficient: to lose this would be unthinkable. That he persists in his inquiries, and risks the consequences, is a measure of the man Francis has created.

Having seen Francis's powerful exposition of violence and his stripping of Sid Halley's soul, the reader is then reminded of his enviable ability to provide something for a complete cross section of readers. At this point he introduces some lightheartedness, with well-researched technical details for good measure. Switching to the search for Jenny's ex-lover, Sid visits a fair at a stately home. Francis reduces the tension by introducing a scene in which a fortune teller tries to read Sid's false hand, culminating in a flight in a hot-air balloon. The latter, the authenticity of which was ensured by the fact that Dick and Mary Francis took just such a trip, is invigorating and lively and includes a marvelous pen portrait of the crazy balloonist John Viking—a man without fear, after Sid's own heart.

It would be unkind to reveal here too many details of the

cases in which Sid is engaged. In that relating to George
Caspar's horses, Francis comes up with a highly ingenious
and scientifically plausible method that has earned *Whip
Hand* the description "almost like science fiction."[19] Often
his books rely for their mystery element upon the criminal's
means of fixing races, an aspect that appears to present Francis with limitless possibilities. It must also be mentioned that,
while the whodunit element is rarely used by Francis, in
Whip Hand there is a surprise for the reader in the case of the
Jockey Club bribery, with all loose ends secured and all expla-
nations completed in a manner worthy of one of the classical
detective novelists.

Sid's relationship with Louise McInnes helps him to
bring normality into his life after his many traumatic experiences, with Louise showing a willingness to accept him at face
value that could never be forthcoming from Jenny. Perhaps
Jenny is a little more understanding after Sid has cleared her
of complicity in the con man's activities, but there is no prospect of a reconciliation.

Much of *Whip Hand* represents a search for self-respect
on the part of Sid Halley. The threats of the criminal force
him to turn tail, then he begins to fight back, but the cold fear
remains with him and no one (least of all Jenny) can be asked
to assist. The very last words round it off perfectly, restoring
to Sid his manhood. Criminals, he discovers, can lose their
nerve too:

> He stood there for a moment, brooding, holding his
> gun; and then he gave me back what in the straw barn
> he'd taken away.
> "Isn't there *anything*," he said bitterly, "that you're
> afraid of ?"[20]

"I want," says Jenny, "an ordinary man." Sid Halley is
hardly that.

4

The Hero as Reluctant Peer, Weary Agent, and Newspaperman

Flying Finish
Blood Sport
Forfeit

Flying Finish introduces with memorable clarity a not-too-reputable firm that transports racehorses by air between England and many other countries. Francis knows flying, his experience dating from World War II; what he does not know is always made good, and for *Flying Finish* he actually traveled on a plane transporting horses in order to get the feel and the necessary technical points.

The narrator is Henry Grey, a young man rebelling against his genteel social background and with no interest in taking advantage of his birthright. A late child born into the aristocracy, he knew from an early age that his parents viewed him only as the requisite heir to the earldom; affection scarcely entered into the matter. "I didn't love anyone," Henry tells us. "I hadn't had any practice."

With such a soulless beginning it is not surprising that Henry rejects their way of life and takes an unimpressive job with a bloodstock agency, while occupying his spare time as an amateur jockey and by taking flying lessons. The members of his family hold all this in predictable disapproval. Henry persists in order to control his own affairs, and not through rebellion of an aggressive nature. Indeed he is a mild and sedate character, as he himself admits:

> A repressed, quiet, "good" little boy I had been, and a quiet, withdrawn, secretive man I had become. I was almost pathologically tidy and methodical, early for every appointment, controlled alike in behavior, handwriting and sex.[1]

The bloodstock agency deals regularly with a firm called Yardman Transport and its manager Simon Searle. Yardman has been suffering of late; two of their employees disappeared in Italy and they are undermanned. In search of a change, and because of his passion for flying, Henry persuades the obsequious Yardman to take him on as a traveling groom.

Henry's new working life is depicted with grim realism. The hard labor of loading and unloading racehorses onto aircraft, the responsibility for their care and comfort in flight, the disagreements that can exist between grooms in this isolated and enclosed situation, are all there for the reader to see. Minor squabbles with lazy and resentful workers fade into insignificance, however, when Henry meets young Billy Watkins. From this point the book becomes a duel between the two men. "For Billy," Henry recognizes, "the class war existed as a bloody battlefield upon which he was the most active and tireless warrior alive. Within five seconds of our first meeting he was sharpening his claws."[2]

The aggression of Billy Watkins is obvious from the outset, in his constant sneers and baiting of Henry and in his sullen insolence:

> He wasn't so much a man, not even so much a person, as a force. A wild, elemental, poltergeist force trapped barely controllably in a vigorous steel-spring body. You couldn't look into Billy's cold eyes from inches away and

not know it. I felt a weird unexpected primitive tingle away down somewhere in my gut, and at the same time realized on a conscious level that friendliness and reason couldn't help, that there would be no winning over, ever, of Billy.[3]

In a strange way Henry can see Billy's point of view about the aristocracy, although it is ironical that Billy should display this hatred toward one who has rejected the trappings of wealth and nobility and the way of life to which he was born. Henry has cast aside the glorious past, and is determined to live in the real world rather than to perpetuate what he sees as the anachronism of the English ruling classes; but Billy is so steeped in prejudice that Henry's thoughts are of no interest to him.

Henry's self-made existence provides him with some uncomfortable experiences while working for Yardman. In addition to being subjected to physical violence by the vicious Billy, he has to cope with a berserk horse at thirty thousand feet. This particular scene, where Henry has no option but to slaughter the animal with a bread knife, is described in detail. It might be regarded as superfluous, but could equally be applauded as a totally reasonable illustration of what could face a man who has chosen to follow this particular occupation. It also serves to emphasize the sacrifices that Henry has made; unlike many people, he has the option of a softer life and has made a conscious decision to decline it.

Francis's characterization, a skill he possesses in greater measure than is generally appreciated, is seen to good effect in *Flying Finish*. Henry Grey himself has something to say, as a privileged person who wants only to be a human being, and Billy Watkins has views that are implanted by a background that might enlist sympathy were it not for the viciousness and brutality with which he asserts his points. Thirdly there is Gabriella, a sales assistant at Malpensa Airport in Milan with whom Henry falls in love, who is presented not as a token rav-

ishing beauty but as a girl of unusual spirit and fascinating interest. Not the least aspect of Gabriella, which Francis uses to
show humanitarianism as well as courage, is her sideline of
providing birth-control pills to the poor women of Milan.
Francis might seem to be playing up the comedy element
when he describes how pilots and stewardesses smuggle the
pills to Gabriella in aspirin bottles, but there is also a poignant
issue involved: her free contraception service began when her
sister suffered a nervous breakdown after bearing six children
in six years.

As Henry remarks, Gabriella is quite a girl. At first he admires her public-spiritedness and her outspoken views, although the language barrier makes communication difficult.
Then a tender relationship grows between them, and they become lovers. But Francis is always adept at the neat joke constructed with few words, and after they have made love
Henry says:

> I thought about her with love and without even the
> conventional sort of anxiety, for she had said with a gig-
> gle, it would be a poor smuggler who couldn't swallow
> her own contraband.[4]

Henry soon discovers that Yardman's manager, Simon
Searle, has been using the flights to collect export grants on
horses that he moves backwards and forwards between England and the continent. Before Henry can take any action,
however, he becomes preoccupied with family affairs upon
the death of his father and his unwanted succession to the
earldom. Searle takes Henry's place on the next flight with
Billy, and fails to return.

To Henry it is inconceivable that this third disappearance of a Yardman employee in Italy could be coincidence.
His impatience to investigate, and also to spend more time
with Gabriella, is heightened by thoughts of the future with

which he is faced as a result of his father's death. It is an important point for Henry, since he was never certain of his ultimate reaction when the day of his inheritance arrived. He has found it impossible to decide if he will renounce it or resign himself to a position and lifestyle alien to his beliefs. To his family, it seems probable that Henry will mature and accept his birthright and its responsibilities: but to Henry, maturity gives him the right to refuse and to lead his own life with Gabriella as a wife, rather than with a carefully selected social equal for purposes of perpetuating the family lineage.

Henry is now determined to discover what has befallen Simon Searle, and he returns to Milan to continue the search with Gabriella. Here he learns that Searle's export racket is but a small-time piece of private enterprise, compared with the larger criminal scheme that is being conducted by Yardman Transport. Dangerous men are involved, and those who stumble upon the truth are removed. This is made clear when Gabriella is shot in the street. Henry leaves her in the hospital in a critical condition, and shortly afterwards is abducted by Yardman and Billy. It is strange that the reader never learns whether or not Gabriella recovers—from this point the book builds up to a frightening climax, and Gabriella is never seen again. Francis appears to invite the reader to supply an ending according to taste. "People often ask me what happened to Gabriella," he says. "Sometimes I like to leave readers something to think about."[5]

The last fifty pages of *Flying Finish* are beautifully paced, an excellent example of Francis's ability to fuse action, menace, and physical violence into an unrelenting line of suspense. Billy shows himself to be far more than a mere enemy of the aristocracy; there is in him a sadistic cruelty, a killer instinct and a contempt for his victims that Francis paints with sickening credibility. He also makes it clear to the reader that it is right for Henry to fight back without mercy, that it is impossible to remain on the side of the angels and observe all

the rules of fair combat when faced with a character like Billy.
It is a moral dilemma that the Francis heroes are frequently
forced to consider.

Flying Finish is an adventure story on the grand scale.
While it is immensely enjoyable and in parts thought-provoking, it is largely escapist entertainment and clearly fiction. In
contrast there sometimes occur events in real life that could
so easily have come from Francis's books. For instance there
was the kidnapping of the racehorse Shergar from the Aga
Khan's stud farm in Ireland on February 8, 1983, which was
leading news in the British press for many weeks. No clear explanation was forthcoming, and the story eventually grew
cold. Bearing in mind the value of Shergar as the 1981 winner
of both the English and Irish Derby, was it a case of kidnapping for ransom? Was the horse dead or alive, still in Ireland
or half a world away? At the time of publication the mystery
remains unresolved. The point to be made here is that many
described it as "just like a Dick Francis thriller." If such a
comparison is correct, then *Blood Sport* is quite probably the
book to which such commentators referred, for it concerns
the disappearance of top racehorses.

There the similarity ends; investigator Gene Hawkins is
fortunately more successful than Shergar's pursuers. The further dissimilarity (as far as is known) is that the horses in
Blood Sport are stolen for a highly ingenious purpose that
will not be revealed here, but that is skillfully contrived by
Francis, and that is more satisfyingly original than the con-
ventional motive of ransom.

Gene Hawkins is a complex character, a man of such
mixed emotions that he nervously sleeps with a Luger under
his pillow yet is indifferent to continuing to live a lonely and
pointless life. The reader is not specifically told of his work,
but is left to assume that it involves national security and that
Gene is already beginning to feel vulnerable and world-
weary:

> Forty still lay a couple of years ahead but I could have
> told Methuselah a thing or two. . . . The day-to-day social
> level had lost all meaning, and underneath, where there
> should have been rock, had opened a void of shriveling
> loneliness. . . . Only work brought my splintering self
> into any sort of whole, and I knew well enough that it was
> the work itself which had started the process.[6]

The pressures of his work, combined with the isolation of his
wrecked emotional life since the departure of his mistress,
have put Gene on the verge of a mental breakdown.

His new interest, proving to be a lifeline that occupies
and shapes his mind, is awakened by his mysterious boss
Keeble on behalf of Dave Teller. Dave is the American part-
owner of two kidnapped racehorses, and Gene's reluctance to
undertake the investigation is overcome when an attempt is
made upon Dave's life.

Most of the action in *Blood Sport* takes place in the
United States—New York, Kentucky, Wyoming, and Ne-
vada—with Francis expanding his horizons and setting the
scene outside his own home territory with authenticity and
feeling. The reader is in America with Gene Hawkins, not just
in an Englishman's idea of America. Whereas some British
writers portray the American people only in stereotype,
which might also be said similarly of some American novelists
writing about England, Francis makes no such mistake and
presents his characters with complete credibility. The pecu-
liarly British flavor of his first few books was, at this early stage
in his career, giving way to the universality that has since
made him a truly cosmopolitan novelist.

Such careful characterization and avoidance of the stereotype are here to be seen in Walt Prensela. Walt is a New
York insurance investigator who is already working on the
case when Gene arrives, and whose initial suspicion turns to
acceptance, respect, and cooperation as the two men begin to
work together.

Francis often endeavors to show the effect of particular lifestyles and events upon individual personality and behavior. Thus the reader is introduced to Dave Teller's English wife and learns—not for the first time in Francis's books—that horses can play havoc with a marriage. "The first bloody thing about horses," she tells Gene, "is that they make bloody fools of men."[7] Eunice Teller is rich, and leads a completely bored existence. On first acquaintance Gene observes her attitudes, coarse language, tendency to drink, and open invitation to bed, and decides that she is a very troubled woman. Her life is empty—as a direct result of having everything she could desire by way of material possessions. Greatly to her surprise and chagrin, Gene later explains to her the reason for her promiscuity after refusing to take advantage of it:

> "Sex . . . this sort of casual sex," I patted the bed where she'd lain, "can be a way of running away from real effort. A lover may be a sublimation of a deeper need. People who can't face the demands of one may opt for passing the time with the other."
> "For Christ's sake, I don't understand a bloody word." . . .
> "Thousands of people never try anything serious because they're afraid of failing," I said.[8]

A nice touch is the revelation that there is more to Eunice than meets the eye, and that her boredom can be overcome by making use of her talents. In short, Gene persuades her that her skills in interior design could fill her life if she made a business of it.

The heart of the mystery lies at a dude ranch in the Rocky Mountains, where Gene books in under an assumed name. From this point the tension builds in typical Francis fashion, with a leavening of humor and character observation as the assorted guests appear.

Gene is fired with a determination not only to expose those responsible for the horse stealing, but also to identify their motive. Since champion stallions of international repute cannot be sold openly, and since no ransoms have been demanded, the criminals' intentions are complex and require a great deal of effort to penetrate. Gene also intends to recover the horses themselves. The advantage swiftly changes as the story moves towards its climax, with Gene's cat-and-mouse game backfiring so that he needs all his guile to stay alive. In the event Gene's decisions, together with a stroke of fate, result in loss of life for which Gene blames himself.

The adventure has nevertheless occurred at a most significant point in Gene's life, a point where his failure of will has become almost irrevocable and the pressures upon his mind have left him suicidal. While his search for the missing stallions provides him with a new impetus, the bloody conclusion makes its mark upon him and Francis leaves the reader with a lingering doubt as to Gene's future.

Like *Flying Finish*, *Blood Sport* is an adventure tale well told, but Francis's claim to distinction is more clearly seen in the book that followed. *Forfeit*, honored with the Edgar by the Mystery Writers of America, is one of Francis's best novels viewed from any angle. The narrator, James "Ty" Tyrone, is a crusading Fleet Street journalist working for a Sunday newspaper with a reputation for exposés. Francis conveys the atmosphere of the Street with great competence, doubtless stemming from his own experience as a columnist for an extensive period following his retirement from racing. He knows how the Street works, and what makes newspapermen tick in the less reputable but popular corners of the trade. What he has to say is not always complimentary, as in Ty Tyrone's cynical description of his walk to the office one morning:

> People hurried along Fleet Street with pinched mean eyes, working out whose neck to scrunch on the next rung of the ladder, and someone bought a blind man's matches with a poker chip.[9]

Yet Francis also displays a softer touch, a tolerance and understanding towards the outwardly hard men of the scandal sheets:

> Derry's desk held a comprehensive reference library of form books in the top three drawers and a half bottle of vodka, two hundred purple hearts, and a pornographic film catalogue in the bottom one. These were window dressing only. They represented the wicked fellow Derry would like to be, not the lawful, temperate semidetached man he was.[10]

Ty Tyrone, like any Francis hero, is a man with problems. Domestically his life is dominated by the fact that his wife Elizabeth is almost totally incapacitated from polio, bedridden and completely reliant upon an electric respirator. Professionally his problems begin on the day a quality magazine commissions him to write a background article on a race called the Lamplighter Gold Cup.

Seemingly unconnected is Ty's chance meeting with the elderly and alcoholic racing correspondent Bert Checkov—a nice character sketch this, albeit fleeting as Checkov dies at an early point in the book when he falls from a seventh-floor window. There is no suggestion of foul play. Paralytic with drink as usual, Checkov stumbles and crashes accidentally to his death, but not before passing to Ty some rambling advice against selling his soul and his column.

While gathering material for an article, Ty meets a beautiful half-caste girl called Gail Pominga. His marital circumstances have forced him to obtain his sexual satisfaction where he can, although the deep shame he feels and his love for Elizabeth have restricted his activity considerably. The seductive Gail, a teacher at a college of art, is an immediately inviting liaison. In an unusually frank and explicit scene for Francis, they make love on first acquaintance.

Ty's first thought afterwards is for Elizabeth:

> The old weary tide of guilt washed back. The world closed in. . . .
> For better or worse, I thought bitterly. For richer, for poorer. In sickness and in health keep thee only unto her as long as you both shall live. I will, I said.
> An easy vow, the day I made it. I hadn't kept it. Gail was the fourth girl in eleven years. The first for nearly three.[11]

The dilemma for Ty is acute. He feels an irresistible urge to meet with Gail regularly, yet he is tied to Elizabeth; not from a sense of duty, but a genuinely loving relationship that makes it necessary for him to deceive her about his infidelity.

Working on his article brings Ty into contact with various racing people who knew Bert Checkov, and gradually a clever plot begins to emerge. Checkov had indeed sold his soul, by agreeing to write laudatory stories about indifferent horses in order to encourage the public to bet heavily on them. The criminals blackmailing Checkov then intimidate the horses' owners to scratch them as runners, thus ensuring that they retain the bettors' cash—hence the book's title, referring to the rule under which ante-post bets are forfeited if a horse is scratched. It is a typically neat device, a small point of racing detail upon which a complex and satisfying plot is based.

Ty's plan is to hide one of the heavily backed horses to ensure that it races as scheduled. This interference, together with some pointed remarks in his newspaper column, inevitably results in drawing the villains into the open. Their leader, a South African named Vjoersterod, is the embodiment of icy menace, a highly dangerous man who has masterminded racing frauds in various countries. First they subject Ty to a vicious beating, then threaten to inform his wife about his affair with Gail. This prompts him to confess to Elizabeth himself, in a scene presented by Francis with great sympathy, the helpless Elizabeth bearing up to the revelation with a strength that hits Ty harder than any emotional outburst might. Quiet tears and a little bitterness are all she displays:

Reason might tell her that total lifelong celibacy was a lot
to demand, but emotion had practically nothing to do
with reason, and the tearing emotions of any ordinary
wife on finding her husband unfaithful hadn't atrophied
along with her muscles. I hadn't expected much else.
She would have to have been a saint or a cynic to have
laughed it off without a pang, and she was neither of those
things, just a normal human being trapped in an abnor-
mal situation.[12]

Vjoersterod ranks as one of Francis's most detestable villains, although he is not the type who personally indulges in
physical torture. He is not in the mold of the sadistic Kraye
who destroyed Sid Halley's hand, but in his way he incurs disgust as justifiably by working upon the fears and emotions of
his victims. This is seen in the methods he uses to intimidate
owners into scratching their horses—he informs one, for example, that unless he complies it will be arranged for his teenage daughter to be raped. Vjoersterod's evil can also be seen
in his confrontation with Ty Tyrone, who by this time has
thwarted Vjoersterod's blackmail by confessing to Elizabeth
and thus leaving it necessary for the villain to devise other
methods of keeping him in line. The menace is all the more
chilling because Vjoersterod rarely resorts to physical brutality:

> "So now we know just where we are, Mr. Tyrone. Did
> you really have the conceit to think you could defy me
> and get away with it? No one does, Mr. Tyrone. No one
> ever does." . . .
> When I still didn't answer immediately, he half turned,
> looked down, and carefully put the toe of his shoe under
> the switch of the electric outlet. From there the cable led
> directly to Elizabeth's breathing pump. Elizabeth turned
> her head to follow my eyes and saw what he was doing.
> "No!" she said. It was high-pitched, terrified. Vjoer-
> sterod smiled.[13]

Vjoersterod's partner Ross is a different proposition. A
systematic beating of Ty with a truncheon is his stock-in-

trade, acquired during his work in a South African prison. Whether intentionally or not, Francis shows a touch of even-handedness in what might otherwise have been seen as a political point. When Vjoersterod refers to Ross's work "in the country I come from," Elizabeth replies: "Russia? Do you come from Russia?"[14]

Gail Pominga, a half-caste African, is similarly in doubt as to Vjoersterod's origins. She detects an antipathetic air about him that she fails to understand. When she tells Ty that Vjoersterod visited her to obtain blackmail evidence against him, she says he spoke to her as if she had crawled out of the cracks. Ty explains that Vjoersterod is South African, and Gail sees the truth—he was posing as someone who was on her side, but he could not hide his prejudice.

Forfeit is a beautifully rounded novel. In addition to the principal plot, with Ty showing obstinacy and grit in conflict with Vjoersterod and his accomplices, Francis introduces a host of minor characters from the world of the turf and presents each one in a skillful little pen portrait. He is never content with cardboard figures or ciphers, but ensures that we are touched, amused, or intrigued by each of them. Vjoersterod's smooth villainy and Ross's brutality remain in our minds, fueled by all the implications of the South African connection without any necessity to be specific. The horror is there: he does not have to spell it out.

Most memorable of all, however, is the triangular love story. The warmth and affection between Ty and the helpless Elizabeth develops into an understanding on her part of his need for sex and a confidence that, whatever he might do, he will always stay with her. Gail knows that Elizabeth will keep him forever. There is no doubt in our minds that both relationships will continue, and that Ty's marriage will survive. Francis seldom leaves such little uncertainty about the future of his characters.

5

The Hero as Victim, Pilot, and Son
Enquiry
Rat Race
Bonecrack

The fact that Dick Francis's steeplechasing career provided authenticity and a wealth of plot ideas for his novels must have proved a mixed blessing to the racing world. On the one hand he avoids the inaccuracies and misinformation that can occur when a special area is treated in fiction by the uninitiated. On the other, his expertise enables him to identify the seamier aspects of racing, the sort of characters who can be an embarrassment to the Establishment, and the occasional unwelcome question that only an insider is in a position to raise. The theme of *Enquiry* falls into the latter category.

Enquiry chronicles two dramatic months in the life of jockey Kelly Hughes. It opens with a deceptively simple statement, which then captures our interest by defining the extent of Kelly's misfortune:

Yesterday I lost my license.

To a professional steeplechase jockey, losing his license
and being warned off Newmarket Heath is like being
chucked off the medical register, only more so.

Barred from race riding, barred from racecourses.
Barred, moreover, from racing stables. Which poses me
quite a problem, as I live in one.

No livelihood and maybe no home.[1]

This summary, together with innumerable incidents revealing the fickle nature of Kelly's friends, provide ample evidence of the effects on a jockey of a sudden and traumatic
disqualification. One can be excused if, knowing Francis's heroes, one instantly believes that Kelly Hughes is *not* guilty
and that all these repercussions are unjust.

Kelly's trainer, Dexter Cranfield, is similarly disqualified
when witnesses testify that Kelly deliberately lost races on
several occasions with Cranfield's connivance, but both men
know that the evidence is false. The utter helplessness of the
accused at the inquiry is demonstrated by Francis with shattering clarity. The strong chairman, Lord Gowery, is flanked
by weak stewards who are willing to be led by him, and he has
clearly made up his mind. The inquiry itself, following established procedure, is held in private and neither heard nor
scrutinized by members of the public or the press. This sti-
fling air of secrecy, with the stewards acting as prosecutors,
judges, and jury, is brought into question most effectively.
Francis illustrates, albeit in a fictionalized and dramatic form
that is perhaps unlikely to occur in reality, the dangers and
unfairness of such an autocratic and outmoded system.

The withdrawal of the licenses of Kelly Hughes and Dexter Cranfield makes the rapid disintegration of both men
seem inevitable. In particular Cranfield, a social climber
whose delusions of superiority are now blunted by thoughts of
what his upper-class friends might feel about him, is shattered
by the likely ruin facing his stables. He is suicidal until Kelly,

encouraged by Cranfield's bored and selfish daughter Roberta, persuades him to pull himself together and work for a future that to Cranfield seems impossible.

Kelly himself is made of sterner stuff, with a resilience and lack of self-pity that stems from the death of his wife Rosalind and her parents in a car crash four years earlier. If he can survive that tragedy, he can keep his head in the current difficulties. Not only is Kelly determined to retain his self-respect and rescue his damaged career, but he has a fierce will to pursue the truth and uncover the plot behind the false evidence laid against him. He begins systematically to break down this evidence, finding that witnesses have been bribed or coerced by an anonymous person, but he is still unable to identify the motive of his elusive enemy.

While tougher than Cranfield, Kelly is still reluctant to impose his presence blatantly upon his friends and colleagues in the racing world. His first instinct is to maintain a low profile, hiding the fact that he winces at the way they look at him, speak to him, or write about him. With a supreme effort, however, he attends the Jockeys' Fund dance at an opulent hotel at Ascot and runs the gauntlet of hatred, bare tolerance, and thinly disguised pity. Roberta Cranfield, redeeming herself by the minute in his eyes, is fortunately there to support him. Indeed it proves to be an occasion on which Kelly not only gets to understand Roberta, but also begins to accept that her brash veneer is something that he has practiced himself. Roberta's snobbishness emerges from their conversation, and Kelly realizes that his own front is equally false:

"You haven't a Welsh accent. You haven't any accent at all. And that's odd really, considering you are only . . ." Her voice trailed away and she looked aghast at her self-betrayal. "Oh dear . . . I'm sorry."

"It's not surprising," I pointed out. "Considering your father. And anyway, in my own way I'm just as bad. I

smothered my Welsh accent quite deliberately. I used to
practice in secret, while I was still at school, copying the
BBC news announcers."[2]

Kelly confesses that he realized the accent of a Welsh farm la-
borer would not have helped him to achieve his early ambition to become a civil servant. The only outcome of his newly
acquired accent, however, was that his parents had begun to
despise him.

Roberta too begins to learn something about herself, that
the social attitudes inculcated by her father must change if
she chooses to be herself rather than what Dexter Cranfield
has made her. Later she reacts bitterly when she discovers
that Kelly's father has sent him a letter steeped in working-
class morality, accusing him of bringing disgrace to the family
by his disqualification.

> "Rigidly moral man, my father," I said. "Honest to the
> last farthing. Honest for its own sake. He taught me a lot
> that I'm grateful for."
> "And that's why this business hurts him so much?"
> "Yes."
> "I've never . . . Well, I know you'll despise me for say-
> ing it . . . but I've never thought about people like your
> father before as—well—*people*."
> "If you're not careful," I said, "those chains will drop
> right off."[3]

Francis has great understanding of how parents and their
social background can have a direct effect upon their off-
spring, producing either mirror images or aggressive rebellion. So often his characters reflect this, for good or ill.

Overcoming the unfriendliness and rejection displayed
at the Jockeys' Fund dance, Kelly persists in his investigation
on the spot and even accosts Lord Gowery. After the dance,
on the drive home, he almost loses his life in a scene that
Francis springs unexpectedly. It is assumed that the danger is

past when Kelly gets out of his car, suffering from the effects
of exhaust fumes. Then it happens: an even greater peril
looms to catch the reader unawares, and Kelly in his stupefac-
tion is unable to recognize the danger himself. At first he
thinks the earth is trembling, and then that the moon is
rushing towards him, before he is jolted into translating this
imagery to a devastating reality:

> Not the moon. A great roaring wailing monster with a
> blinding moon eye. . . . A monster racing to gobble me
> up, huge and dark and faster than the wind and unimagin-
> ably terrifying. . . .
> I didn't move. Couldn't.
> The one-thirty mail express from Paddington to Ply-
> mouth plowed into my sturdy little car and carried its
> crumpled remains half a mile down the track.[4]

Kelly's investigation is beginning to worry his enemies,
and his pressure has caused them to tamper with the exhaust
of his car. He is making progress, but his success will remain
limited while the powers-that-be are ranged against him.
Francis's plot carries the implication that a rigged inquiry is
unlikely to be exposed by one of racing's smaller men, and
Kelly has to approach a titled steward who believes in him
sufficiently to stand up to Lord Gowery.

It gives little away to reveal that Gowery is the victim of
blackmail. To salve his conscience, he has actually begun to
believe that the false evidence sent to him is proof of the guilt
of Kelly and Cranfield. Gowery's indiscretion, which has
placed him in the blackmailer's power, is something that will
not be tolerated by the racing Establishment but is greeted
with surprising equability by Kelly himself. The friendly Lord
Ferth, who has broken Gowery down and unearthed his secret, recounts it distastefully:

> "He says he belongs to a sort of club where people like
> him can gratify themselves fairly harmlessly, as they are

all there because they enjoy . . . in varying forms . . . the
same thing." . . .
"Which is what?" I said matter-of-factly.
He said, as if putting a good yard of clean air between
himself and the word, "Flagellation."
"That old thing!" I said.
"What?" . . .
"Boots and whips and naked bosoms?"
Ferth shook his head in disbelief. "You take it so
coolly."
"Live and let live," I said. "If that's what they feel com-
pelled to do, why stop them? As he said, they're not
harming anyone, if they're in a club where everyone else
is the same."[5]

Kelly's sympathetic attitude is remarkable, in view of the
treatment Lord Gowery has meted out to him. It shows the
tolerance of the modern thinking man, as opposed to the racing aristocracy.

Enquiry is in many ways a genuine detective story, a description that can be applied to few Dick Francis novels. Even
when Kelly has discredited the inquiry and been reinstated
with his license, there remains the mystery of the person or
persons behind the conspiracy. It is a whodunit with a neat
double twist at the climax, but it is more than a thriller or a
puzzle. *Enquiry* encourages us to examine our attitudes to social class and the inclination, whether perverse or necessary,
to reject our own roots. It also leaves the reader in little doubt
of Francis's personal views on the inquiry system, its failings
and its vulnerability to manipulation. This novel cannot have
been welcomed in some quarters.

Having dealt with the shortcomings of the racing Establishment in *Enquiry*, Francis next turned to entirely fresh
ground in *Rat Race* by producing a fast-moving adventure
story about a taxi-plane pilot, with elements in the Alistair
Maclean tradition. The attitude of the narrator, pilot Matt
Shore, gives the book its appropriate title. He is content

enough ferrying passengers to the races for a small firm called
Derrydown, but has lost his ambition to survive the rat race
and taste success in his life. His initiative has been depressed
by his earlier experiences, and this has brought about "a per-
manent state of mind . . . and no discernible joy anywhere."[6]
When an unwelcome acquaintance in a bar visualizes him as a
hell-raiser who beats up the skies and lives the life of a high-
powered gypsy, Matt reflects grimly upon the truth:

> The best thing a pilot can be is careful: sober, meticulous,
> receptive, and careful. There are old pilots and foolish
> pilots, but no old foolish pilots. Me, I was old, young,
> wise, foolish, thirty-four. Also depressed, divorced, and
> broke.[7]

Matt lives a simple existence in the firm's caravan, stav-
ing off the amorous advances of the boss's niece and facing
constant reminders from his ex-wife about overdue alimony.
His divorce, coupled with financial ruin, has left him in a
shell, shunning close relationships and involvement in other
people's affairs. He wants only to be private and cold. Like
Sid Halley in *Odds Against* and *Whip Hand*, he cannot con-
ceive how love can curdle and turn to hate. At times he experiences an urge to pull his life back on course, but fails to re-
spond to it.

So in spite of the popular image of a pilot, Matt's life is
relatively unexciting. On the day he takes off with a group of
racing people bound for Newbury, Haydock, and Newmarket, there are clearly ill feelings between his passengers and
there is some needling at the racecourses from pilots of a rival
airline, but Matt keeps his own counsel. It is all of little significance and concern to him, until his aircraft—fortunately
just vacated by Matt and the passengers—is completely destroyed by a bomb.

The explosion is the turning point in the book. Totally inexplicable, and following Francis's meticulous buildup of all

the characters involved, it is the subject of a scrupulous Board
of Trade investigation but also prompts Matt to make his own
inquiries. Suddenly he develops an instinct for self-preserva-
tion; he comes alive, knowing that the official investigators
have not excluded the theory that he might himself have been
responsible for planting the bomb, or at least that he knows
more than he is willing to admit. From his record he appears
feckless and unreliable—resigned or dismissed from various
airlines, convicted of gross negligence for which someone else
was actually responsible, suspected of gunrunning, trying his
hand at crop-spraying, now in charge of an aircraft that is
wrecked in criminal circumstances.

As always, one feels that Francis knows his subject. In
this case the book is as much about small-time flying as about
racing, and he puts some concise and trenchant comments on
the subject into the mouths of his characters. One example is
the cynical Board of Trade investigator:

> "Aviation will never need a special police force to detect
> crime. Everyone is so busy informing on everyone else.
> Makes us laugh, sometimes. . . . There are no permanent
> friendships in aviation. The people you think are your
> friends are the first to deny they associate with you at the
> faintest hint of trouble. The cock crows until it's hoarse,
> in aviation."[8]

Then there is Matt Shore, bitterly reflecting upon the economic knife-edge on which the aviation industry rests and in
which governments play a decisive make-or-break role. It is
just such snippets of fact or of philosophy that help to give
each of Francis's novels their authentic bite.

It is not only in the short descriptive passages and
snatches of dialogue that Francis creates precisely the right
mood. His longer action sequences, and his introduction of
scientific and technical details, are also competent and satisfying. In *Rat Race* the reader is in effect treated to a lecture on

the operation of a bomb, technically precise but chilling in its implications. When Francis turns to action and pace, this time he proves himself as accomplished in the air as on the racecourse: in *Rat Race* there are no heart-stopping steeplechases, but there is the brilliant passage described by H. R. F. Keating as "an in-the-air rescue sequence that would make you really and truly angry if you had to put it down."[9]

As he responds to the dangerous situation created by others Matt Shore begins to come out of the reclusive attitude into which financial and marital misfortune has placed him. He is also attracted to the sister of a famous jockey, who was traveling in the ill-fated plane, and begins with reluctance to start a new personal relationship:

> The old inner warning raised its urgent head: don't get involved, don't feel anything, don't risk it.
> Don't get involved.[10]

One of his reasons for ignoring these inner warnings is that he feels shame. The girl has a sister suffering from leukemia, whose innate cheerfulness shows Matt that self-pity should not be indulged in by those who can do something to help themselves.

The mystery of who planted the bomb in the plane is solved quite early in the story, but a bigger mystery remains. Who was the intended victim? What was the motive? And above all, who is the person behind the plot? The central idea is a cleverly conceived swindle, which in turn leads to murder and a dramatic climax as innocent people are placed in peril by the ruthless killer Matt has exposed. Along the way the reader meets a carefully balanced cast of characters, all credible human beings. They range from the members of the happy Ross family, living contentedly with the sentence of death that Midge Ross's illness forces them to face; Annie Villars, trainer of racehorses; Chanter, the repulsive hippie who is Matt's unlikely rival for Nancy Ross's affections; the villains, cold and calculating; to the Duke of Wessex, rich and easily led, excitedly playing model trains with his nephew while the villains make him the scapegoat in their murderous fraud. There are many other memorable characters, although the center of our interest is the complex Matt Shore and his return from an emotional grave.

Francis is a writer whose books invite clichés from the reviewers, yet it must be agreed that *Rat Race* is one to be read at a sitting—and perhaps reread, to savor his less obvious skills that are overlooked on the first compulsive pleasure trip. It is very much an adventure story, a description that cannot be applied to its successor *Bonecrack*. Here Francis was again breaking new ground, with a relatively simple plot in which human relationships dominate and action is far less evident than usual. *Bonecrack* is an account of a war of attrition between two men; it examines the themes of monomania and the generation gap.

If economy of words is a feature of Francis's writing, and of that there can be no doubt, then the opening of *Bonecrack* is a good example:

> They both wore thin rubber masks.
> Identical.
> I looked at the two identical faceless faces in tingling disbelief. I was not the sort of person to whom rubber-masked individuals, up to no good, paid calls at twenty to midnight. I was a thirty-four-year-old sober-minded businessman quietly bringing up to date the account books at my father's training stables in Newmarket.[11]

Rather like the racecourse cry of "they're off !" there is no hanging about. In these first few lines the reader is introduced to the narrator, the location, the purpose of his being there, and the totally unexpected predicament he faces. It is not known what the masked men want of him, but Francis dares the reader not to continue and learn more. He is not an elaborately descriptive writer, and is the first to admit it, but his style is highly effective rather than lazy or unliterary.

Neil Griffon, the management consultant whose labors are so aggressively interrupted on page 1, is temporarily in charge of his father's training stables while Griffon Senior is in the hospital following an automobile accident. He knows little about managing stables, nor is he competent to train race-horses, but he can rely upon the head stable lad Etty Craig who is firm, experienced, and the only woman holding such a position on the male-dominated Newmarket scene.

Abducted by the masked men and brought before a Mafia-type figure called Enso Rivera, Neil finds that his hos-pitalized father was the intended victim; he has been taken by mistake. Enso's extortion, of a highly unique variety, is there-fore directed at Neil instead. The demand is to employ Enso's eighteen-year-old son Alessandro as a jockey, and prepare him to ride the stables' best horse in the Derby. The threat, to be carried out if Neil fails to cooperate, is the destruction of the stables.

It is the *means* employed by Enso Rivera to achieve his ends that provides the book with its added and particularly horrifying dimension. This is revealed at an early point, when Enso demonstrates to Neil that he means business; his method, which gives the book its forbidding title, is to break the bones of horses and cause them to be destroyed.

Young Alessandro, who arrives at the stables each day in a chauffeur-driven Mercedes, immediately shows himself to be arrogant and selfish. With the backing of his father, he has complete confidence that he controls the situation and that his every whim will be obeyed. His unwillingness to be bound by the rules of apprenticeship, or to undertake cleaning and grooming duties, breeds antagonism between Alessandro and everyone with whom he comes into contact. For his part, Neil feels that he is betraying Etty and the lads by concealing the hold that the Riveras have over him and that forces him to give Alessandro preferential treatment.

The taut relationship between Neil and Alessandro, which develops and changes as the book progresses, is the focal point of the story. Comparably gripping as a twin theme is the question of the generation gap, and the gulf that can exist between father and son. Francis explores this with feeling in the case of Neil and Neville Griffon. When Neil visits his father in the hospital, he reflects upon his unhappy past:

> He had not been a kind father. I had spent most of my childhood fearing him and most of my teens loathing him, and only in the past very few years had I come to understand him. The severity with which he had used me had not, after all, been rejection and dislike, but lack of imagination and an inability to love. He had not believed in beating, but he had lavishly handed out other punishments of deprivation and solitude, without realizing that what would have been trifling to him was torment to me. Being locked in one's bedroom for three or four days at a time might not have come under the heading of active cruelty, but it had dumped me into agonies of humiliation and shame; and it had not been possible, although I had tried until I was the most repressed child in Newmarket, to avoid committing anything my father could interpret as a fault.[12]

Having left home when he was sixteen, Neil lost contact with his father for fourteen years before seeking him out to make peace. His reception was so cool that Neil, although resuming his family link, did so only to the extent of calling on his father a few times each year. Their relationship barely improved:

> His manner to me was still for the most part forbidding, critical, and punitive, but as I no longer depended solely upon him for approval, and as he could no longer lock me in my bedroom for disagreeing with him, I found a perverse sort of pleasure in his company.[13]

Not even his accident and his involuntary reliance upon Neil has done anything to dilute Neville's authoritarian air or his hurtful lack of trust and confidence, which seems from his thoughtless remarks to amount occasionally to open contempt. His impatience when Neil fails to find someone to take over the training license temporarily, choosing to assume the role himself, can be seen as particularly unfair. It is more unfeeling than even Neville realizes, since he is unaware of what Neil is having to do in order to ensure the survival of the stables.

Apart from a good basic idea in the story line and a smattering of Francis-style tidbits of information about wine and antiques (the interests of Neil and his mistress Gillie), the appeal of *Bonecrack* lies largely in these personal relationships. The reader is encouraged to question, perhaps more than usual, what motivates the characters to behave towards each other as they do. The comparative lack of action, far from being a disadvantage, is clear evidence that Francis produces thrillers for the thinking reader rather than ephemeral vehicles conveying vicarious excitement.

Neil's rebellious independence from his father has given him a strength of character that enables him to withstand pressures rather than remain the underdog. Neil meets the bullying and nagging of Neville from his hospital bed with calm confidence rather than anger, yet Neville persists in the mistaken belief that he can secure a victory. Even when Neville begins to appreciate the efforts Neil is expending on his behalf at the stables, if not the reason for them, Neil knows that gratitude and humility are not in his nature. "The day my father thanked me," Neil tells himself categorically, "would be the day his personality disintegrated."[14]

Neil's determination not to be dominated also begins to have an effect on Alessandro Rivera, so that there are isolated moments when the youngster drops his mask of surliness and

his air of arrogant superiority. At such moments Neil begins
to understand him, almost to sympathize with him:

> It was a pity, I thought, that he was as he was. With a dif-
> ferent father, he might have been a different person.
> But with a different father, so would I. And who
> wouldn't.
> . . . Fathers, it seemed to me, could train, feed, or
> warp their young plants, but they couldn't affect their ba-
> sic nature. They might produce a stunted oak or a luxuri-
> ant weed, but oak and weed were inborn qualities, which
> would prevail in the end. Alessandro, on such a horticul-
> tural reckoning, was like a cross between holly and deadly
> nightshade; and if his father had his way the red berries
> would lose out to the black.[15]

There is therefore an interesting point of comparison between
the incongruous soul mates Neil and Alessandro, both the
products of their fathers' influence, but in Neil's case he has
long cast off the shackles and become his own man. For Alessandro there is far to go, and Francis shows how the ties of
money and fear begin gradually to weaken as Alessandro finds
much in Neil to admire and to emulate. He is increasingly
willing to confide in Neil the problems of communicating with
his father Enso, while Neil ruefully contemplates the parallel
of his own situation:

> "You have met my father," he said. "It isn't always
> possible to tell him things, especially when he is angry.
> He will give me anything I ask for, but I cannot talk to
> him." . . .
> Enso would give Alessandro anything he wanted,
> would smash a path for him at considerable trouble to
> himself, and would persist as long as Alessandro hun-
> gered, but they couldn't talk.
> And I . . . I could lie and scheme and walk a tightrope
> to save my father's stables for him.
> But talk with him, no, I couldn't.[16]

Slowly Neil accumulates evidence against Enso Rivera, while Alessandro displays a conscience about his father's cruelty after two horses have been maimed. Neil and Enso, Alessandro observes with mounting resentment, have been engaged in a power struggle with himself as the pawn in the game. Alessandro's yearning, Neil detects, is for freedom; and this is the one thing that Enso will not permit him, the one item more precious than wealth and expensive chauffeur-driven cars, the one element that Neil himself had snatched at the age of sixteen.

A sickening physical attack on Neil, and the earlier injuries to the horses, have been carried out by thugs under Enso Rivera's direction. Enso's motive is ostensibly to ensure that Neil gives Alessandro all he requires in the world—to ride a Derby winner. When Enso starts to realize that his son wants something more, and that Neil's own rebellion against tyranny is encouraging Alessandro to follow suit, there is a dreadful promise of tragedy as Enso senses his son slipping away from him.

The conclusion mounts to a scene of bloodshed that, witnessed by Alessandro, provides him with the final terrible twist and leaves him with a whole new set of values. It is not possible to finish the book without feeling some of Neil's emotional involvement. In a novel in which crime is not the key factor, Francis shows himself to be a mature commentator on human strengths and frailties. What is more, he can present his views in a manner that is not clinical or disinterested, but perceptive and compassionate.

6

The Hero as Movie Star, Detective, and Bloodstock Agent

Smokescreen
Slayride
Knockdown

By this stage critics were regarding Francis as among the modern greats in the adventure/crime field, with *Time* magazine going so far as to place him "in the company of writers like John Buchan, who created a highly personal genre and then used it, beyond sheer entertainment, to express a lifetime's accumulation of knowledge and affection."[1]

From his early thrillers set in the English racing scene, he had moved with developing confidence to the occasional story with an international flavor, and now he was certainly attracting an international audience. He was further to take these forays into the field of the intercontinental adventure story, while retaining the essential Englishness that is an important part of his success.

A good example of this, *Smokescreen*, opens with a neat piece of sleight-of-hand. Edward "Link" Lincoln is handcuffed to the steering wheel of a trendy sports car, stranded in the middle of a sun-drenched wilderness, the culmination of a

three-day ordeal. Having begun to share his torment, and to
fall victim once again to Francis's seemingly effortless ability
to involve the reader in his hero's struggles and desperate attempts to extricate himself, one learns with a jolt that this is a
location scene in Spain for a new film! Link is an international
movie star.

In fact Link's public image as an all-action tough guy is in
direct contrast with his own self-assessment. He is a very private person, shuns interviews and publicity appearances unless unavoidable, and would be the first person to question his
own courage. Not the rabble-rouser or the playboy, he lives
quietly with his family in a secluded spot in Berkshire, and
like many Francis heroes has a particular tragedy to bear—a
mentally retarded daughter, her condition the result of a fractured skull and meningitis sustained in babyhood.

Francis shows the difficulties for a public figure like Link
in handling such a situation in his own way, so that his family
might enjoy a normal life away from prying eyes. Link is
strongly motivated to ensure the complete separation of his
domestic life and its sadness from his public life and its apparent glamor.

Link's public persona and private life nevertheless begin
to become inextricably entwined when he receives an impas-
sioned plea from Nerissa, the aunt figure who made his otherwise unhappy childhood bearable. The owner of a string of
racehorses in South Africa, Nerissa asks Link to find out why
they are running so badly. She is a dying woman, bravely facing her end, but desperately worried that she might be leaving her nephew Danilo a worthless legacy if the mystery of
her failing horses is not cleared up. Although surprised and
amused that Nerissa should see him as a resourceful and cou-
rageous adventurer, Link feels compelled to help her and flies
to South Africa, taking advantage of the fact that one of his
films is about to open there. This in itself presents him with a
problem, since he maintains his insistence upon privacy and

refuses to give newspaper interviews or appear on television talk shows.

On arrival in Johannesburg, Link is met by Clifford Wenkins, the nervous and damp-palmed distribution manager for Worldic Films. Throughout *Smokescreen* Francis maintains a sharp yet repulsive character study of this harassed pawn in the publicity machine, pathetically anxious for Link to make personal appearances and give the media men all they require, and frightened almost to the point of tears that his employers will hold him personally responsible for Link's resolute refusal. It is a clear indictment of the system that decrees that figures like Link belong to the public, body and soul, while figures like Wenkins exist to pressurize them to fulfill this obligation.

As with any Francis novel, there are elements to satisfy a wide variety of readers. The story line is clear, well developed, and with numerous twists. Added to this, however, is the factual data, fascinating glimpses into matters that form the background for the principal story. The reader learns some of the intricacies of horse racing in South Africa, the machinery of film-making and the soul-selling demanded by the publicity monster, and most impressively the technical details of gold mining.

With a South African setting, it is to be expected that some discussion of apartheid occurs. On this subject Francis is evenhanded, although he is not tempted into the irrelevance of introducing it as a major issue. This is consistent with his other novels, where political questions play little part— with the possible exception of *Trial Run*. It cannot be assumed from this that Francis does not hold views of his own, but he obviously does not regard his novels as vehicles in which to expound them; there is no message, no mission to lecture to his vast international audience. In *Smokescreen*, Link takes a neutral stance when faced with newspaper reporters in Johannesburg who are eager to provoke a contro-

versial remark. He protests that he has no view to offer about
their political scene, since he is a newcomer to the country
and has not observed it at first hand, but they continue to
press him:

> Well, what were my views on racial discrimination? I
> said without heat that I thought any form of discrimina-
> tion was bound to give rise to some injustice. I said I
> thought it a pity that various people found it necessary to
> discriminate against women, Jews, aborigines, American
> Indians and a friend of mine in Nairobi who couldn't get
> promotion in a job he excelled at because he was white.[2]

Francis also gives one of his characters an opportunity to
explain at some length the South African viewpoint:

> "It means living separately," she said. "It doesn't mean
> that one race is better than the other, just that they're dif-
> ferent, and should remain so. All the world seems to
> think that white South Africans hate the blacks and try to
> repress them, but it is not true. We care for them . . . and
> the phrase, 'Black is beautiful' was thought up by white
> Africans to give black Africans a sense of being important
> as individuals."

Those who attack the régime, claims this advocate, will only
encourage intransigence rather than change. Then, sounding
rather like an official press release couched in conversational
English, she continues:

> "It slows down the progress our country is gradually mak-
> ing toward partnership between the races. The old rigid
> type of apartheid is dying out, you know, and in five or
> ten years' time it will only be the militants and extremists
> on both sides who take it seriously. They shout and
> thump, and the foreign press listens and pays attention,
> like they always do to crackpots, and they don't see—or
> at any rate they never mention—the slow quiet change
> for the better which is going on here."[3]

Link's inquiries are barely advanced before an attempt is made on his life by means of a sabotaged microphone, and later he survives a further attempt in the depths of a gold mine. This latter passage is a good example of Francis's skill in developing tension step by step; Link is separated from his party, then finds himself in darkness except for the menacing light from his attacker's helmet, and finally has to feel his way out of the mine before blasting operations commence. Leading up to the excitement of the tight spot in which the central character finds himself, Francis feeds us copious technical details about gold and its extraction, although one character cynically pierces the fallacy of the situation with flawless reasoning:

> "What is gold for, though? This is what we should be asking. What everyone should be asking. What is the *point*? Everyone goes to so much trouble to get it, and pays so much for it, and it has no real *use*. . . .
> "Everyone digs it out of the ground here and puts it back underground at Fort Knox, where it never sees daylight again. . . . Don't you see—the whole thing is *artificial*? Why should the whole world's wealth be based on a yellow metal which has no *use*?"[4]

So it is evident that someone wants Link dead. Has he unwittingly made progress in the matter of Nerissa's horses, or might there be another reason? Link believes he knows the answer, and the book's title is a fair indication of the truth.

It is nevertheless some time before Link is able to expose the criminal, and he has to survive a gruelling ordeal manacled in a car in the most desolate area of the Kruger National Park—a carbon copy of the book's opening scene, this time genuine rather than a film shot, and an ironical fusion of Link's public and private beings. It is a good piece of descriptive writing and an ideal vehicle for Francis's style of first-person narrative. The reader experiences with Link, painfully and inexorably, the appalling heat, thirst, cramp, swollen

limbs, bodily stench, physical exhaustion, and the descent towards insanity.

This final torturous experience forces Link, the private
man, to become the Link of the public image in order to survive. It is revealing nothing to say here that he succeeds in
this, trapping his adversary in the process. He succeeds not
only as a man of courage and grit, a role that for Link has
previously been confined to celluloid, but also excels as a detective.

Another detective, this time in the true sense of the
word, is narrator David Cleveland, of *Slayride* (*Slay-Ride* in
Britain), who is an investigator for the Jockey Club. David is
in Norway, working with his opposite number Arne Kristiansen on the case of British jockey Bob Sherman, who has disappeared together with a day's takings from Øvrevoll racecourse. It is clear from the beginning, with a literally chilling
murder attempt in a fjord, that someone is reluctant for the
investigation to make much headway. Routine inquiries made
by David with Sherman's contacts among the Norwegian racing fraternity are not met with universal friendliness, and it
appears that little progress is in the offing. The situation is not
assisted by the arrival in Oslo of Sherman's wife Emma, five
months pregnant and degenerating emotionally towards total
breakdown.

There are various indications, not least the unsuccessful
attempt on his life, that persuade David to view Bob Sherman
as dead. The missing money amounts to less than Sherman
might make by remaining for some top races, and he is unlikely to have been able to transport heavy bags of coins. David's feeling, therefore, is that Sherman's body is still in the
vicinity of the racecourse.

The eventual discovery of the body, after much fruitless
searching and the dragging of a pond, is described by Francis
with macabre brilliance and simplicity.

The boy didn't move, but he said something which
halted my three companions in mid-step. They stood literally immobile, as if their reflexes had all stopped working. Their faces looked totally blank.
"What did he say?" I asked.
The boy repeated what he had said before, and if anything the shock of my companions deepened.
Baltzersen loosened his jaw with a visible effort, and
translated.
"He said, 'I have found a hand.' "[5]

The six-year-old boy, scavenging around the empty racecourse for money dropped by the crowds, has made the grisly
discovery that gives rise to his simplistic statement, and upon
which Francis then elaborates:

> The child was not mistaken. Waxy-white and horrific, it
> lay back downwards on the tarmac, fingers laxly curled up
> to meet the rain.
> What the child had not said, however, was that the
> hand was not alone.
> In the angle between the wall and the ground lay a long
> mound covered by a black tarpaulin. Halfway along its
> length, visible to the wrist, the hand protruded.
> Wordlessly the senior policeman took hold of a corner
> of the tarpaulin and pulled it back. . . .
> He was unrecognizable really: it was going to be a teeth
> job for the inquest.[6]

The corpse has clearly been removed from the pond by
someone before the commencement of dragging operations,
with the intention of returning it later. This itself indicates a
criminal with inside knowledge of the progress of the investigation and the police search. Nevertheless at this point David
has achieved his mission to find Bob Sherman, and the murder is a matter for the Norwegian police. His work finished,
he escorts the debilitated Emma back to London.
David's attitude changes abruptly when it appears that

the case is pursuing him, and that he will be unable to opt out of it. First Emma is viciously attacked by thugs whom she has surprised in the act of ransacking her house; as a result, she loses her baby. Then David is attacked in his own flat. His return to Norway in search of the solution is his overt reaction against the physical assault he has suffered, but there is also a stronger inner reason:

> I supposed that no one who hadn't seen her as I had could properly understand all that she'd suffered; and I knew that it was in great part because of Emma that I was back in Norway. No one should be allowed to inflict such hurt on another human being, and get away with it. The fact that the same agency had murdered Bob and tried to see me off was in a curious way secondary: it was possible future victims who had to be saved. If you don't dig ground elder out of the flower beds, it can strangle the garden.[7]

Again David's presence in Norway is frostily received by the racing Establishment, but the police are cooperative if uninformative. Through the police David is introduced to the impecunious author Erik Lund, who acts as his driver during his stay. A madcap motorist, left-wing conversationalist, purveyor of facts and gossip concerning the racing notables who figure as David's suspects, and master of an enormous Great Dane called Odin who provides some hilarious moments, Lund turns out to be another memorable character well drawn by Francis.

Arne Kristiansen and his wife Kari are also skillfully presented. They share a settled relationship but have fallen out of love, at least in Kari's case. Arne is no longer on top of his job as investigator for the Norwegian equivalent of the Jockey Club, since he has assumed a persecution complex and is in constant fear that he is being followed or that his conversation is being bugged. This attitude is plausibly explained as a repercussion of events in World War II, the shooting of his grandfather and the overpowering influence of his father's dangerous existence in the resistance movement. His constant edginess, combined with his passion for loudly playing Beethoven records when he is upset, are recurrent and moving themes throughout the book. Kari is sensual, a lover of life, increasingly frustrated. This last point becomes obvious to David Cleveland when she dances with him, in what is probably the most erotic passage of any Francis novel:

> I knew theoretically that a woman could reach a vivid orgasm without actual intercourse, that in fact some could do it when all alone simply by thinking erotic thoughts, but I had never before seen it happen. . . .
> Her breathing grew slower and deeper and her eyes lost their brightness. Her mouth was closed, half smiling. Head up, neck straight, she looked more withdrawn and absent-minded than passionately aroused. Then quite suddenly her whole body flushed with heat, and behind her eyes and right through her very deeply I was for almost twenty seconds aware of a gentle intense throbbing.[9]

When one considers that eroticism and blatant sexuality are rarely employed by Francis, this is extreme. Nevertheless he uses it to depict in a few paragraphs Kari's tensions and illicit emotions arising from Arne's psychological problems.

The remainder of the book shows David Cleveland in relentless pursuit of the killer, traceable through an item secreted by Bob Sherman and eventually discovered by David. When he finally identifies his enemy, David is compelled to chase hired henchmen who are in search of a key witness, the endgame being played against a stunning scenic background replete with menace. *Slayride* is a thriller and a mystery, but the way in which the danger is accentuated by the environment gives it a clear relationship to the sort of outdoor adventure tales that Francis is known to admire.

It also requires minimal scratching beneath the surface to

reveal in *Slayride* some thoughtful themes of more than passing interest. One of his favorites, the lack of understanding between father and son, recurs here in the Sandviks. More importantly, however, the reader observes how the actions of various men today can be heavily influenced by attitudes of mind and reflexes developed during wartime in an occupied country; how their bravery at that time, and their finely tuned cunning against the aggressor, later become the driving force of their criminality and their rebellion against the legitimate legal authorities of today.

Yet Francis's undoubted success in the field of the international adventure thriller—and more were to come, with *In the Frame, Trial Run,* and *The Danger* in particular—did not prevent him from returning to the home-based racing mystery he had made his own. In *Knockdown* (*Knock Down* in Britain), very much on tried and tested ground, he continued to show that his fund of tricks and nefarious schemes on the English racing scene was far from exhausted.

His protagonist, Jonah Dereham, is a bloodstock agent working in the world of racehorse sales. He buys at auction on commission for rich clients, has an expert eye for a potential winner, and makes many enemies among those who live by rigging the sales and inflating or deflating prices. Like many a Francis hero, he has his personal crosses to bear. In Jonah's case the problems are twofold, adding to the dangers and traumas of the adventure in which he becomes unwittingly involved—he has a shoulder that dislocates at the slightest provocation, and he has an alcoholic brother, both of which prove to be vulnerable targets for men who would put pressure on him.

An honest man in the milieu of bloodstock sales is a rare phenomenon in *Knockdown*, with Jonah conspicuously unique in this respect. "The sales ring scenes," as reviewer Philip Pelham remarked, "are hair-raisingly convincing."[9] While Francis does not deliberately mislead the reader into assuming the worst about all who operate in this field, since in spite of his frequent air of almost documentary authenticity one is still aware that the story is fiction, he is inclined to place disquieting words into Jonah's mouth:

> I chewed the end of my pencil and thought about the bloodstock jungle which I had entered with such innocence two years earlier. It had been naïve to imagine that all it took to be a bloodstock agent was a thorough knowledge of horses, an intimate relationship with the studbook, hundreds of acquaintances in the racing industry, and a reasonable head for business. Initial surprise at the fiddles I saw all around me had long since passed from revulsion to cynicism, and I had grown a thick skin of self-preservation. I thought that sometimes it was difficult to perceive the honest course, and more difficult still to stick to it, when what I saw as dishonesty was so much the general climate.[10]

Jonah is himself the typical good guy of the Dick Francis world, literally the honest broker, a man who will retaliate if provoked or will fight to protect his security and the principles in which he believes, but a man who will not seek to win in the rat race by manipulating the gullible or by overpowering the weak.

A memorable aspect of *Knockdown*, leaving one sad and angry, is the sympathetic handling of the problem of alcoholism. Jonah's brother Crispin, with whom he was orphaned and who now shares his home and sponges intolerably upon him, at first appears as an unlovable character; but his actions can be seen as pathetic rather than willfully aggressive. Arguments with Jonah and demands for money and drink easily turn to tears of self-pity and childlike promises to reform, to be broken with an inevitability that Jonah has come to expect. But it is not Crispin himself who leaves the reader feeling angry at the conclusion; it is the discovery that others have fed his illness as a weapon against Jonah, that the final result is tragedy, and that Crispin has been misjudged rather than understood.

Francis paints a depressingly credible picture of the alcoholic and what it is like to share his life. His bouts of insensibility, his rapidly changing moods between belligerence and cloying affection, his loss of appetite, his physical sickness, are all symptoms that Jonah meets with brotherly love rather than repulsion.

The main plot concerns the fixing of bloodstock auction prices, linked with demands for money kickbacks from the vendors; alternatively, if the vendors do not cooperate, the opposite system applies and prices are deflated by the spreading of rumors about the horses' state of health and prospects. A vendetta is being waged against Jonah for refusing to participate in the racket, and he is the victim of thuggery designed to ruin his business. Like many a stoic Francis character, he reacts by choosing retaliation rather than capitulation and sets out to smash the racketeers.

In this Jonah is assisted by Sophie Randolph, of all things a lovely air traffic controller still pining after the death of her lover, together with her redoubtable horse-breeder aunt Antonia Huntercombe. The latter is what is popularly known as a tough old bird, who has suffered financially at the hands of the crooked bloodstock agents and now wants to hit back.

When the intimidation extends to burning Jonah's house, and he rescues Crispin from the flames, it provokes another bout of self-pity:

> Blaming me for not letting him die was his way of laying all his troubles at my door. It was my fault he was alive, his mind went, so it was my fault if he took refuge in drink. He would work up his resentment against me as a justification for self-pity.[11]

In essence *Knockdown* is a study in retaliation. The methodology of the racketeers is to single out the strong and honest man, then to apply pressure to bring him to heel. Jonah shocks his tormentors by fighting fire with fire, and he defeats them with his own released aggression. "Bash me, I bash back," is the phrase he continually employs, then later adds ruefully to himself: "The way wars started, big and small." Indeed Jonah's war finally surprises even himself, when he realizes that he is prepared to kill and resists the impulse only with difficulty.

7

The Hero as Toymaker, Artist, and Accountant

High Stakes

In the Frame

Risk

Although not one of Francis's stronger plots, *High Stakes* is interesting in its exploration of human relationships and in its exposition of the many ways that easy money can be made in the racing game. Its starting point is a breakdown of trust, a shattering revelation to an honest man that he has been gullible. Steven Scott, the storyteller, owns nine horses that have been trained by his close friend Jody Leeds. It has been a partnership that has produced winners, but the perfect relationship suddenly crumbles when Steven discovers that Jody and an apparently respectable bookmaker called Ganser Mays have been systematically cheating him of thousands of pounds.

Steven's disbelief is an understandable first reaction. He is stunned by the revelation that the long friendship has been false, and there is no way of repairing it or of forgiving Jody for his actions. He takes the only clear course open to him, and removes his horses from Jody's care.

Francis has created some intriguing characters in *High*

Stakes. Steven himself has become a rich man from the invention and patenting of children's toys, which gives Francis ample opportunities to catch the reader's interest with some well-researched technical details. Then there is his friend Charlie Canterfield, a self-made businessman with a mind like a razor, whose humble beginnings have inspired him to achievement and wealth—the working-class lad made good, a recurrent theme of Francis. A concise but meaningful picture of the man defines in a few words what makes him tick:

> I'd seen it in him before, this split-second assessment of a new factor, and I knew that therein lay the key to his exceptional business acumen. His body might laze, his bonhomie might expand like softly whipped cream, but his brain never took a moment off.
> . . . Charlie had never hidden his origins. Indeed he was justly proud of them. It was simply that under the old educational system he'd been sent to Eton as a local boy on Council money, and had acquired the speech and social habits along with the book learning. His brains had taken him along all his life like a surf rider on the crest of a roller, and it was probably only a modest piece of extra luck that he'd happened to be born within sight of the big school.[1]

One of the most entertaining characters in the entire Francis canon is Bert Huggerneck, the big man whose interest in food is based upon quantity rather than culinary niceties, and who is determined to even a score with Ganser Mays. Bert was a bookie's clerk until his employer, swindled by Mays, lost control of his business to him. Together Steven, Charlie, and Bert set out to uncover the elaborate rackets of Jody Leeds and Ganser Mays, and it becomes evident that Steven's losses are the tip of the iceberg where these manipulators of horses and betting systems are concerned.

Part of Francis's skill lies in his ability, without laboring the point, to ensnare the reader in the misfortunes and frustrations of his central characters. *High Stakes* is a good example of this, as the reader experiences Steven Scott's difficulties in convincing anyone that he is on the side of the angels. Jody Leeds is highly respected, with his father firmly ensconced in the higher echelons of the racing Establishment, and Steven's aggressiveness towards him is seen as ingratitude and arrogance by the press and the public. Moreover when Leeds and Mays begin deliberately to destroy Steven's credibility by framing him for drunken driving, Steven is forced to fight back in order to retain his own reputation.

In the world of Dick Francis, the villains rarely seem able to assess the true mettle of the stoical heroes, the quiet men who are galvanized into action by a sense of outrage at what has been perpetrated. While these heroes often share the simple philosophy expressed by Jonah Dereham in *Knockdown*—"You bash me, I bash back"—it is more than a straightforward desire for revenge, and they have about them almost a knight-errant quality, a mission to ensure that the evildoers are deprived of the opportunity to harm others. In the case of Jody Leeds, Steven feels at the outset little more than a deep sense of betrayal, although it proves necessary for him to wage war when he discovers that Jody has retained his best horses and returned "ringers" to him. In the case of Ganser Mays, one can detect in Steven a more disinterested motive, the determination to stop him for the protection of the weak:

> From Bert Huggerneck's description of the killing off of one small bookmaking business, it was probable Ganser Mays had as much professional honor as an octopus. His tentacles stretched out and clutched, and sucked the victim dry. I had a vision of a whole crowd of desperate little men sitting on their office floors because the bailiffs had taken the furniture, sobbing with relief down their telephones while Ganser Mays offered to buy the albatross of their lease for peanuts: and another vision of the same

crowd of little men getting drunk in dingy pubs, trying to
obliterate the pain of seeing the bright new shop fronts
glowing over the ashes of their closed books.[2]

As the battle against Leeds and Mays progresses, Francis
concocts a fine mixture of menace and humor. The humor
comes largely from an elaborate scheme to beat the villains at
their own game of horse swapping, involving a complex cha-
rade and "Box and Cox" routine while a number of horses are
in transit; this sequence shows ingenuity in Francis, as well as
his ability to produce an effect almost of farce. Steven's plan is
also cleverly likened to the toys he invents, when "all the little
pieces will rotate on their spindles and go through their al-
lotted acts,"[3] although the villains are unaware that he is
playing with them. This imagery has been remarked upon
elsewhere,[4] but after the fun one is back in the serious world
of criminality where the villains pursue revenge and security
by stooping to horse killing. The climax is exciting and terrible, as it becomes evident that the loss of the battle and their
fortunes can have the effect of pushing criminals over the border line into insanity.

High Stakes is solid and dependable, if somewhat standard Francis fare. Flexible as ever, he returned after it to the
international scene with In the Frame, showing again how
crime can extend to such proportions that its ramifications can
be felt in continents half a world apart. In doing so he firmly
exposed as falsehood the suggestion that he merely writes
thrillers about horseracing, by producing a plot in which
there is only the barest connection with the sport. Indeed the
assertion can be made that the racing element is coincidental,
and might well have been introduced to satisfy those readers
to whom a Francis novel without it would be somehow incom-
plete—a feeling Francis himself recognizes to exist among his
public.[5]

One of his standard literary ingredients is in effect defined on the first page of *In the Frame*. "I stood on the outside of disaster, looking in," are the opening words of narrator Charles Todd, and the reader knows that very shortly Todd will be on the inside—albeit a reluctant hero, responding to unsought circumstances and events. Charles is a painter who happens to specialize in equestrian subjects, although for the purposes of the plot it would matter very little if his theme were landscapes or still life. It is the world of art that holds the center stage of *In the Frame*, and this is a fine example of Francis's ability to combine scrupulous research with wholly enthralling storytelling.

Charles Todd arrives at the Shropshire home of his cousin Donald Stuart with the expectation of a pleasant weekend stay; instead he finds the house ransacked, Donald's young wife Regina battered to death, and Donald himself under suspicion of her murder. Francis shows great capability in handling such a situation with compassion, and in presenting the shattered figure of Donald, broken down by grief at his personal loss and stunned by the insinuations of the police.

Francis has often depicted police officials as unsympathetic. The businesslike and unfeeling approach of investigating officers, at least until subsequent events prove them wrong, is to be seen in *Dead Cert, For Kicks, Knockdown*, and *Banker* as well as *In the Frame*. In all cases the victims of crime are treated as suspects, perhaps indicating that the narrator's role as free lance investigator affords him the luxury of believing in the less obvious solutions to the mysteries concerned. Nevertheless it is an interesting point that in the works of Dick Francis, policemen are rarely wonderful.

The problem for Donald Stuart is that all his most valuable possessions disappeared at the time of his wife's murder, that this could, conceivably, be an insurance swindle on his part that went wrong. Among his missing treasures is a painting by Munnings, purchased by him on a recent trip to Australia. Charles Todd has reason to recall this fact when, soon

afterward, he meets a rich middle-aged widow whose house
has been destroyed by fire after being burglarized—one of
her missing items being a Munnings that she, too, brought
back from Australia.

The widow, Maisie Matthews, is a delightful creation. A
dressy and bejeweled example of the nouveau riche, she is
surprisingly unpretentious in her speech and mannerisms and
is outrageously open in the confidences with which she approaches Charles on their first acquaintance. Maisie is totally
credible, outwardly happy-go-lucky in the face of adversity,
but occasionally betraying the fact that a briefly happy and
comfortable existence as a rich man's second wife has left her
lonely and a trifle disoriented since his death. It is little wonder that Charles immediately warms to her and determines to
investigate the misfortune that shares common factors with
that of Donald. The chance meeting between Charles and
Maisie might itself be an unlikely coincidence, but such devices can be forgiven if not overemployed by the thriller
writer, and in this case the meeting provides the spark that
activates the entire plot.

Financed by Maisie, Charles flies to Sydney to investigate and stays with Jik Cassavetes, an old friend from art-
school days. Once a bohemian rebel, Jik now lives on a boat
with his slightly disapproving wife of three weeks; he joins
forces with Charles, but faces the continuous conflict between
his lingering recklessness and the more sober demands of his
newfound domestic responsibilities. When it seems that they
are beginning to catch up with the perpetrators of the Munnings fraud, the details of which are still a mystery, Sarah sees
the potential danger to Jik and criticizes Charles for proceed-
ing further. His answer typifies the reactive nature of the normally peaceable Francis hero:

> "Sure," I said. "Anyone who tries to right a wrong these
> days is a fool. Much better not to meddle, not to get in-
> volved, not to think it's your responsibility. I really ought

to be painting away safely in my attic at Heathrow, minding my own business and letting Donald rot. Much more sensible, I agree. The trouble is that I simply can't do it. I see the hell he's in. How can I just turn my back? Not when there's a chance of getting him out. True enough, I may not manage it, but what I can't face is not having tried."[6]

Charles is concerned not only for Donald Stuart. He is concerned also for Jik, who retains the outlook on life that Charles affectionately recalls from their student days, but is in danger of losing under Sarah's influence.

A pity about Sarah, I thought. She would have Jik in cotton wool and slippers if he didn't look out; and he'd never paint those magnificent brooding pictures any more, because they sprang from a torment he would no longer be allowed. Security, to him, would be a sort of abdication; a sort of death.[7]

Such perceptive glances at the differences between human beings, and how people can change, are the means by which Francis delineates his characters. They do not affect the pace of the action or the story line, which, in the case of a thriller-writer, can be maintained quite adequately without making the characters anything more significant than pieces on a chessboard to be moved around at will. This does not satisfy Francis: he cares enough for his craft, and thinks enough of his readers, to breathe some life into his characters and give them some identifiable feature or something worthwhile to communicate.

The remainder of *In the Frame* is a menacing cat-and-mouse operation, with Charles and his friends (Sarah gradually unfreezing and becoming committed to the task) uncovering evidence of a huge international racket, in which the cases of Donald Stuart and Maisie Matthews turn out to be but two among many. By means of deception and guile, together with a spot of breaking and entering, Charles exposes an organization involved in art forgery, robbery, arson, and murder on a grand scale. A favorite device of Francis—that of having the cats suddenly become the mice as the criminals retaliate to silence their pursuers—is used in a way here that develops the tension systematically to the final pages.

In the Frame is arguably the nearest the author has moved towards the detective-story format—a step-by-step accumulation of evidence with a climax in which the principal villain is unmasked. This structural advance, plus the technical details of painting he learned from professional artists and galleries, again demonstrates that Francis is never content to rest upon his laurels, to produce time and again the sort of racing thriller which relies only upon his personal experience.

His versatility and willingness to experiment has resulted in a high overall quality in his novels, but it would be strange if there had not been occasional patches of unevenness. Of course he possesses certain abilities that can be clearly identified in every book he has written, but the one aspect in which he cannot always be a winner, and the one that governs all in terms of the overriding impression made upon us when reading any popular fiction, is the plot itself. In the field of adventure stories, thrillers, or mysteries—describe his work how you will—the plot or central idea is of supreme importance. *High Stakes* has already been identified as lacking a strong plot, and one regretfully reaches the same conclusion about *Risk*. Indeed these two works would epitomize Francis's less satisfactory period were it not for the fact that they were separated by the excellent well-plotted *In the Frame*.

Such criticism must be placed in context, since it did not prove to mark the threshold of a "pot-boiling" period or the exhaustion of Francis's ideas; nor has he ever lapsed into a tired succession of weak imitations of earlier successes. Thus it is worth stressing that the slightly disappointing plots of *High Stakes* and *Risk* foreshadowed no lasting significance and should be viewed as aberrations, since in subsequent years he produced some of his very best work.

The central character of *Risk*, Roland Britten, is a chartered accountant who adds the spice of excitement and danger to his life by riding in steeplechases as an amateur. One of the morals of the story is that Roland probably does not need to be a jockey in order to bring the element of risk into what might appear to be a dull and methodical existence. His financial acumen has been responsible for exposing more than a few irregularities, some deliberate frauds, and a monumental swindle involving local government building projects that has sent the perpetrators to jail. With Roland's enemies now thirsting for revenge, steeplechasing is child's play.

The action begins when Roland is kidnapped after winning the Cheltenham Gold Cup and he is held prisoner on a boat. For a substantial part of the book, Francis treats us to a craftsmanlike account of a man in solitary confinement. Roland's mind is in turmoil. He is unaware of the identity of the person who has engineered his abduction and of his captor's ultimate intention towards him. The first-person narrative is used most effectively here, enabling the reader to feel with Roland his bewilderment, discomfort, and mounting frustration as time passes.

After stretching to the full his mental and physical faculties, Roland eventually escapes, following twelve days' incarceration, suffering from the disorientation caused by the dramatic change from his state of limbo to his reentry into the real world. With his newfound freedom, he has regained the ability after a long silence to communicate with another human being. His escape finds him on the island of Minorca, and there he shelters in the hotel bedroom of an unlikely angel of mercy:

> She matched her voice: a no-nonsense middle-aged lady
> with spectacles and a practical air. Self-confident. Tall: al-
> most six feet. Thin, and far from a beauty.[8]

Francis's economical description introduces Hilary Margaret Pinlock, a girls' school headmistress on vacation. Further described as "a fulfilled career woman of undoubted power," she is not the first positive female character to appear in Francis's books; nevertheless she makes a more direct impact upon the protagonist than is generally the case. Indeed she provides something of a shock by propositioning Roland without preamble, quite clinically and decisively. "Will you go to bed with me?" she asks, leaving Roland utterly speechless until he finally prompts her, and receives a strange explanation:

> She half-smiled, ruefully. "It's been in my mind, now and again, for a long time. You will find it extraordinary, but I have never . . . so to speak, slept with a man." . . .
> "So why *now*?"
> "I hope you won't be angry . . . but it is mostly curiosity, and the pursuit of knowledge."[9]

Roland agrees, although Francis leaves us uncertain as to his reasons. There is no suggestion that he finds Hilary attractive, in fact quite the reverse is true. Could it be that there is an element of gratitude for providing him sanctuary? Again this is unstated. It is far more likely that he accepts and responds to Hilary's explanation of her need for sexual intercourse. She feels that she has now reached the age where it has become unattainable, yet she has to cope with highly sexed teenage girls, to deal with sex education, and to assist them with their problems—including unwanted pregnancies. As a spinster, not only does she sense a lack of respect from the girls themselves, but also a patronizing attitude on the part of the married members of her staff.

Whatever Roland's reasons it is a most unusual situation, quite unparalleled in Francis's other novels:

> It was the strangest love-making, but it did work. I looked back afterward to the moment when she first took

pleasure in the sensation of my stroking her skin; the rip-
ple of surprise when she felt with her hands the size of an
erect man; the passion with which she finally responded;
and the stunning release into gasping incredulity. . . .
    "Oh my goodness," she said in a sort of exultation. "So
now I *know*."[10]

This is sex without either lust or love. To many it might
seem a totally superfluous passage, but it is presented with
sufficient skill to incline one to disagree with the comment by
Alex de Jonge that "the writer seems more at home in the
weighing room than in the bedroom."[11] At the very least it
shows the care taken by Francis to build a character. Hilary
could so easily be a token figure, flitting into and out of the
story merely for the purpose of helping Roland out of his difficulties. Instead Francis shows us a woman grappling with a
very real problem of her own, desperate for sexual experience
and with a credible reason for being so. The author identifies
a contemporary dilemma, which eschews mere titillation and
provides one with food for thought about today's permissive
society and the pressures upon those who have adhered to the
standards of the past.

    Francis is the complete master of pace, as any successful
jockey must be. Knowing when to hold back and when to
surge forward is a vital element in a well-run and well-
planned race, and his novels display this knack admirably. A
change of pace occurs in *Risk* when Roland parts from Hilary
and returns to England, moving from a quiet and thought-
provoking passage to an arrival home that immediately finds
him in physical danger. It is clear that someone is still seeking
him out, determined to do him harm.

    While a lesser man might choose to spend the rest of his
life looking over his shoulder, wondering in terror when the
next attack or abduction is to occur, Roland is inclined to hit
back. He shares the agonizing question experienced by Sid
Halley in *Whip Hand*—capitulate? live in fear? or take up the

challenge? Sid's anguish and his short-lived surrender are caused by a precise threat by a known adversary, but Roland's situation is frightening because of its very mysteriousness. His enemy has not identified himself, nor revealed the reason for his enmity.

Francis shows Roland to be the sort of man who will not take the assault upon him lightly, who will not buckle under. The police are not interested, since there is no clear evidence that a crime has been committed, so Roland must obstinately root out his anonymous enemy himself. At first one might think he is strangely atypical as a chartered accountant, but Francis shows that first impressions can be deceptive. While Roland's chosen career might indicate a tendency towards security and steady employment, and while pedantry and staidness might be the popular conception of the accountant, his enthusiasm for risking his neck as an amateur steeplechaser gives the lie to this. Indeed it is revealed that even his entry into accountancy was motivated by the fact that his mother committed suicide after receiving bad financial advice. So Roland is a man of reforming zeal, a man of action, and once again a Dick Francis villain has underestimated the worth of a Dick Francis hero.

Roland pursues his investigation, assisted by Hilary Margaret Pinlock, and as their inquiries develop so too does their relationship—a touching platonic friendship in contrast to their first love-making, and with many small indications deftly planted by Francis to show that Hilary now has confidence in herself as a woman and no longer needs sexual experience to complete the picture. Eventually Roland's adversary is exposed, though not before a further abduction, incarceration, and release.

Risk is a mystery story, with suspects ranging from those previously convicted by Roland's evidence to people who wish to conceal their current financial transgressions from his scrutiny. Roland's investigation—to determine if his abductor is motivated by revenge or by insecurity—is a routine affair by Francis standards. Nevertheless the book poses various challenges to Francis as a novelist, to which he responds well. The complex characters and relationship of Roland and Hilary, together with the influences working upon them, are skillfully conveyed. So too is the trauma of solitary confinement, with a disturbing exposition of Roland's frustration at finding himself indefinitely deprived of his liberty and his ability to communicate. These features alone make *Risk* a worthwhile and imaginative book, even if it is short on some of the other qualities expected by the typical Francis enthusiast.

8

The Hero as Envoy, Photographer, and Duo
Trial Run
Reflex
Twice Shy

Setting a novel in Moscow was a brave departure for Dick Francis. In many ways *Trial Run* is a further example of the sort of tale in which he had already proved himself a master. There is a horse-racing background, and the fact that the action occurs some fifteen hundred miles from his home ground was by this time hardly calculated to raise an eyebrow—his protagonists had, after all, traveled much further afield in *Blood Sport, Smokescreen,* and *In the Frame.* The main difference on this occasion is that his ex-jockey Randall Drew finds the danger in what is in some respects the ultimate in foreign countries, while Francis evokes the atmosphere of Moscow itself with great feeling to convey the potentialities of diplomatic conflict. Amid his brooding air of intrigue and menace, there is little left untouched—least of all horse racing—by the destructive hand of the political process.

Randall Drew himself is a reluctant adventurer. He has an enjoyable and unfettered relationship with his blonde

girlfriend Emma, who supplies most of the excitement in his
life since he retired from steeplechasing because of poor eye-
sight and began a placid but restless existence as a farmer.
There is no way in which he can be likened to James Bond; on
the contrary, he instinctively refuses the mission to Moscow
that people in high places are attempting to press upon him.
Some similarities nonetheless exist between Randall Drew
and Sid Halley. While it is true that Sid is more the man of action than Randall, this largely stems from necessity; he is a
private detective by profession. Randall is less likely to place
himself on the firing line, although he has to admit that his ev-
eryday life has become humdrum. This is where the likeness
to Sid can be seen, for Randall's career as a jockey has similarly been demolished by a physical stroke of fate—with Sid it
is the loss of a hand, with Randall the less serious but equally
damning affliction of astigmatism. Randall is also bronchitic
and asthmatic, which are not impossible odds for a jockey but
are hardly advantageous.

Thus while Sid Halley has a terrible physical incapacity,
and while Randall Drew does not suffer the traumas of displaying an obvious external deformity, both men share the
frustrations of knowing that they will never race again. Sid has
nightmares about it, while Randall merely faces boredom and
yearns for a part of his life that is dead. This in itself must be
an incentive to take up the potentially exciting offer to go to
Moscow on a mysterious errand for the Foreign Office, but
still his instincts are against it.

In *Trial Run* Francis pictures the British convention that
the social pecking order creates people who know their place
in society, and conversely breeds rebels against tradition
and class. Randall's girlfriend Emma is in fact Lady Emma
Louders-Allen-Croft, described as the daughter, sister, and
aunt of dukes. She first appears in jeans, check shirt, baggy
sweater and cowboy boots, but her rebelliousness goes much
deeper. She is, in her own words, "into the working girl
ethos."

She was employed full time, no favors, in a bustling London department store, where, despite her search for social abasement, she had recently been promoted to bed linen buyer on the second floor. Emma, blessed with organizational skills above the average, was troubled about her rise, a screw-up one could trace back directly to her own schooling, where she, in an expensive boarding school for highborn young ladies, had been taught in fierily left-wing sociology lessons that brains were elitist and that manual work was the noble path to heaven.[1]

Randall, in contrast, is more of a traditionalist. He is also more inclined to accept that there is a social order decreeing that some people are born to rule, and that others are born to do or die. Hence it proves possible to persuade him to go to Moscow by the simple expedient of bringing in a person of even higher status: this is a prince, no less than the cousin of the monarch. Randall capitulates. Emma's reaction is predictably tart:

> It's too ingrained in you. Service to the sovereign, and all that. Grandfather an equerry, aunt a lady-in-waiting. Stacks like them in your family for generations back. What hope have you got? When a prince says jump, all your ancestors' genes spring to attention and salute.[2]

Another reason for Randall's initial reluctance to become involved is the very vagueness of the mission. The prince's brother-in-law, Lord Farringford, is likely to be selected to ride in the forthcoming Moscow Olympics, but rumors are circulating that he will be at risk. There is the possibility of embarrassment to the Royal Family and a major diplomatic incident stemming from an unknown source; the powers-that-be feel it essential to identify this source before making a decision about Farringford's participation. These rumors begin to assume some foundation, and Randall's interest is aroused, when Farringford tells him of a physical assault upon him by two men who warn him to "keep away from Alyosha."

This is the basic mystery posited in *Trial Run*—who or what is Alyosha? Lord Farringford himself is singularly uninformative, and he appears genuinely to know little, although the sparse data he has been able to acquire arose from circumstances that as a close relative of royalty he is unable to broadcast. Nevertheless he has to admit confidentially to Randall that the shadowy threat against him stems from his friendship with Hans Kramer, a member of the German equestrian team who died of a heart attack at the Burghley horse trials. Farringford had ill-advisedly accompanied Kramer to a transvestite club, although he had been misled into believing it to be merely a gambling den. At Kramer's death, rumors started circulating that he and Farringford were having a homosexual affair, and that a certain Alyosha from Moscow was sufficiently jealous to pressurize Kramer into a heart attack. Farringford hears a rumor, far removed from its original source, that if he ever goes to Moscow, Alyosha will be waiting.

Thus one of the staple ingredients of the espionage thriller appears in Francis's work for the first time, albeit flavored with his expert knowledge of equestrian matters and the added twist that Randall is dealing with threats to the aristocracy and national security at the highest level, rather than with the more usual faceless men of the intelligence services. The basic assumption of much espionage fiction is that anyone going to Russia is vulnerable, but a potential scandal arising from a royal personage's alleged sexual propensities is on an entirely different scale; Randall's task is not only to assess the likelihood of political capital being made but also to thwart the voracious appetites of Fleet Street's gossip columnists.

To any reader, the dilemma might appear to be quite easily avoided. Any danger to the nation could be minimized if Farringford were merely to decide not to go to Moscow. But the interesting point being made by Francis is that a member of the Royal Family is like any other person, with the common citizen's individual ambition and desire to shine in a chosen field so as to reflect credit on self and country. "I want a Gold," Lord Farringford says, in one simple statement epitomizing his own aspirations even more than his patriotism.

Randall's exploits in Moscow are determined largely by the conventions of the espionage novel—there is a game being played; nobody knows the nature of the game or the intended result; with the sole exception of Randall there is no player in the game who can be trusted to maintain allegiance to one side or the other. Francis displays a neat hand in depicting Russian contacts in the world of horses, cool ladies from Intourist, heartily apolitical or politically ardent travelers from England, and Foreign Office plants in Moscow institutions. All give the impression, as the writer hopes, that they might not be what they seem. It is often said with humor that espionage novelists of the le Carré school present to the reader a labyrinth of double-dealing and a dramatis personae that can be comprehended only after careful study. Here in *Trial Run*, but in a less earnest vein, Francis proves that he too is no mean exponent of the form.

Francis spins a web of confusion for the reader who, identifying with Randall Drew, finds frustration mounting as contacts are made, information is extracted from men who are continually glancing over their shoulders, and everything leads back to the keyword Alyosha. The identity of Alyosha remains a closely guarded secret until the climax. Randall is certain only of the fact that Alyosha spells death and that the death of Hans Kramer was a trial run in murder that was to be the precursor to many others. On three occasions he narrowly escapes death himself.

It is a beautifully constructed novel, replete with peaks of suspense and troughs of social and political comment, the whole integrated by a plot of which the big "blockbuster" writers of international intrigue stories would not be ashamed. The Russian setting gives Francis the opportunity to comment upon the atmosphere and way of life in this most perplexing of countries. He completed the book immediately after visiting Moscow himself, and thus approaches the task with authenticity and honesty. By nuance and with incidents pertinent to the plot, and carrying the credibility of a man with no political axe to grind, he conveys the repression that stems from insecurity. What is more, by drawing the reader into the atmosphere that Moscovites regard as normal, he enlists our sympathies for the common man rather than disgust for the oppressors and the bureaucrats. One character tells Randall that there is no telephone directory in Moscow, and that directory assistance will want to know why he needs a number before deciding if it should be given to him; another refers to the lack of unemployment, because so many people are employed to form small groups of watchers at airports, bus shelters, and hotels. Randall soon forms his own impressions of the weariness of the ordinary people, the shortage of the necessities of life, and the cowed spirit of a great city; he expresses them succinctly and sadly, in passages like these:

> He, too, had the inexpressive face and unsmiling eyes which were the Moscow norm. Mobility of features, I supposed, was something one did or didn't learn in childhood from the faces all around; and the fact that they didn't show didn't conclusively prove that admiration and contempt and hate and glee weren't going on inside. It had become, I dared say, imprudent to show them. The unmoving countenance was the first law of survival.[3]
>
> "What is the queue for?"
> "Boots. Warm boots, for winter." . . .
> "But it will take you all day," I said.
> "Yes. I need boots. When boots come in shop, everyone come to buy. It is normal. In England, the peasants have no boots. In Soviet Union, we are fortunate."
> She walked away . . . and attached herself to the end of the patient line. The only thing that I could think of that England's bootless peasantry would so willingly queue all day for would be Cup Final tickets.[4]

Francis gives us a picture of emptiness, but does not fall into the trap of predictably casting the Russians and their system as the only villains. Randall unearths an international terrorist plot in which, if it were to be successful, Russia would be the loser as much as any country in the free world. The highly trained youthful fanatics of anarchistic movements are seen in *Trial Run* to be a force that is equally dangerous to all systematically organized societies, irrespective of whether those societies fall into the neat pigeon holes of democracies or antidemocracies.

Randall, face to face with the proponents of hate and terrorism, sees them as the products of their age. They represent the rebellion of youth against their parents and the imperfect world they have created, with the rebels' scorn turning to anger and to anarchy. From that point, motivation is lost and criminality takes over:

> And after that, the deeper, malignant distortions. . . . The self-delusion that one's feelings of inadequacy were the fault of society, and that it was necessary to destroy society in order to feel adequate. The infliction of pain and fear, to feed the hungry ego. The total surrender of reason to raw emotion, in the illusion of being moved by a sort of divine rage. The choice of an unattainable end, so that the violent means could go on and on. The addictive orgasm of the act of laying waste.[5]

Trial Run is one of Francis's finest books. It might even be his best to date, but such phrases are subjective. Whenever a new Francis novel appears, at least one reviewer is inclined to hail it as his best ever. This creates the impression that each Dick Francis novel is better than all that has gone before it, and that impression is, of course, false. It is unfortunate that the inevitable unevenness within an output of twenty-four novels is rarely recognized, for on the first occasion that a new Francis novel receives uniformly indifferent reviews it will provoke speculation that his peak has been reached and only a slippery downward slope lies ahead. It must therefore be honestly accepted that some of his books have been better than others, that there has been no steady upward graph of excellence, that even in the less satisfactory books there are features of merit, and finally that he has never yet written a book that is actually bad.

Having stressed the realities of the situation, it is no contradiction to state that his last few books have been in a class of their own. The next in the impressive recent sequence is *Reflex*, a story in which racing figures largely but is equally balanced by the technology of photography. Its many qualities fully justified the award of another Edgar by the Mystery Writers of America.

One of the key characters of *Reflex* has died before the story opens. He is George Millace, a professional photographer specializing in racing pictures, the candidness of whose work made him few friends among the jockeys, trainers, and owners he deflated. The narrator, Philip Nore, is a young jockey who is himself passionately interested in photography, and who remembers Millace with bitterness:

> George Millace, pitiless photographer of moments all jockeys preferred to ignore, was safe in his box and appropriately at that moment being lowered underground to his long sleep. And good riddance, I thought uncharitably.
> . . . One might have at least tolerated his debunking approach but for the cruelty sliding out of his eyes. He had been a mental thrower of banana skins, lying in wait to scoff at the hurt; and he would be missed with thankfulness.[6]

Thus the reader recognizes at the outset the antagonism felt by Philip toward Millace, the natural resentment of one engaged in a highly skilled and dangerous occupation who sees another prepared to capitalize upon the inevitable accidents and errors that occur. One senses also, however, that Philip's own knowledge of photography has given him a degree of grudging admiration for Millace's professionalism, since Millace could only have made his reputation by producing a superb if unpalatable result.

Francis's narrators are almost invariably men with problems, and not merely the problems arising from the villainy of others. Philip Nore has problems to spare. His first arises when his dying grandmother, a rich woman from whom he has been estranged since childhood, bluntly informs him that he has a half sister who was born after Philip was abandoned by his mother many years before. The old woman wants to make the half sister her heir and asks Philip to trace her. Not surprisingly, since he blames his grandmother for causing his troubled childhood by rejecting his mother and all her appeals for moral and financial support, Philip wants nothing to do with the matter.

His second problem arises from the insecurity of his job. Although staidly content with average success in steeplechasing, his rides will only continue if he follows the instructions of trainer Harold Osborne and owner Victor Briggs. Since their instructions frequently involve the deliberate throwing of races to benefit themselves financially, and since Philip is essentially an honest man who is becoming increasingly reluctant to compromise himself in this way, his future career looks uncertain. Philip's own view of his career is philosophical and simple:

> Most people think, when they're young, that they're going to the top of their chosen world, and that the climb up is only a formality. Without that faith, I suppose, they might never start. Somewhere on the way they lift their eyes to the summit and know they aren't going to reach it; and happiness then is looking down and enjoying the view they've got, not envying the one they haven't. At around twenty-six I'd come to terms with the view I'd reached, and with knowing I wasn't going any further.[7]

The experiences of Philip's childhood have conditioned his outlook on life, as well as framing his independent spirit and providing the unusual spin-offs of an interest in photography and a yearning to ride horses. Having been rejected by the ramrod-willed grandmother, Philip's mother committed him to a strange and unsettled existence:

> I had never actually lived with my mother, except for a traumatic week or two now and then. We had had no house, no address, no permanent base. Herself always on the move, she had solved the problem of what to do with me by simply dumping me for varying periods with a long succession of mostly astonished married friends, who had been, in retrospect, remarkably tolerant.
>
> . . . It was an extraordinary, disorienting and rootless existence from which I emerged at twelve, when I was dumped in my first long-stay home, able to do almost any job around the house and unable to love.[8]

Spells of living with two photographers and a racehorse trainer gave Philip his particular passions, but did little for his security or his need for stable and lasting relationships. Even as he changed from the disturbed child to the more independent man, he was left with the aching gap of never really knowing his mother.

Philip's third problem concerns a mystery in which he has no particular desire to become involved, but into which he is impelled by his passion for photography. Following George Millace's death in a car crash, which seasoned Francis readers will immediately suspect to be more than meets the eye, the Millace house is ransacked by intruders. It is clear that they are looking for something Millace has cleverly hidden, and Philip's conviction that incriminating evidence is to be found in Millace's rubbish box of old films and prints poses a challenge to his technical know-how.

So Philip Nore has arrived at a turning point in his life. He must deal with all the problems that have erupted, and he must progressively unlock himself from the prison of uncertainties and influences in his own past as surely as he must unlock the secrets of Millace's ingenious photographic puzzles. In crime fiction one may be forgiven for sometimes wondering why the heroes do the things they do. Often it is simply that they are paid to do them, being private investigators or policemen. Sometimes they are just inquisitive or bold men or women of action who choose to involve themselves in a mystery or seek a brush with danger. Francis's investigators are normal people, rarely larger than life, who are caught up in circumstances to which they must react; cases have already been mentioned where the driving force is self-defense or retaliation against an aggressor, but sometimes there are deeper influences at work. Philip Nore in *Reflex* is an example of a man taking stock of his life at a particular point and deciding that he need not remain a victim of his past.

Philip's would-be associate in his search for his half sister is Jeremy Folk, a young solicitor; in certain respects Jeremy is a soul mate, being the junior partner in a family firm and lacking the confidence of his grandfather and uncle. At first Philip remains adamant but he is influenced by an involuntary feeling of sympathy towards the beleaguered Jeremy and by the need to fill the gaps in his own mind. There is also the very persuasive fact that Philip has never known the identity of his father, and this secret is being kept by his grandmother until such time as she has secured his cooperation. As a result of all these irresistible forces, Philip and Jeremy begin to work together and in the process build a close relationship that later sees Jeremy risking his life by also investigating with Philip the Millace affair.

Simultaneously Philip's dilemma with Osborne and Briggs is reaching a flashpoint, since the new forceful Philip is unwilling to lose any more races for them. His blank refusal of their demands is all that is required, a determination to stand up to them and to face the consequences:

When had I changed . . . and how could it have happened without my noticing? I didn't know. I just had a
sense of having already traveled too far to turn back. Too
far down a road where I didn't want to go.[9]

Another satisfying aspect of *Reflex* is the skill with which
Francis takes the reader systematically through the cracking
of George Millace's photo puzzles. Francis has to assume that
his readers have little or no knowledge of photographic processes, whereas Millace has concealed evidence with the ac-
complishment of an expert and it can only be unearthed by
means of photographic expertise. Philip Nore does so, guiding
the ordinary reader through highly complex techniques without blinding them with science. It is all genuinely exciting
without being tediously technical. Francis communicates the
thrill of the chase within the confines of a darkroom, and we
feel as rewarded as Philip feels when a picture of blackmail
begins to emerge.

When the facts about George come to light, with ramifications involving several of Philip's acquaintances in and
around the racing scene, Philip learns never to take people at
their face value. In particular he begins to understand Millace
himself, and it is ironic that the man's death leads to a reas-
sessment of his character that could not take place while he
lived. Similarly, as Philip discovers the details of his own family background, he again finds his long-held misconceptions
undergoing a transformation and providing him with the
satisfied mind that for years he never realized he lacked. Indeed Philip, his long-lost half sister, and others with whom he
comes into contact in his search, have been appropriately described as "the grown-up survivors of the English sixties."[10]

All this is achieved in one of Francis's best novels in
terms of construction, with everything dovetailing neatly for
the involved reader. There is an abundance of crime, but it
seems almost incidental to this smoothly narrated account of
one man in search of his own past and another man's secrets.

Philip Nore is a well-executed study of a man and what makes him the way he is. There are nevertheless those who level against Dick Francis the criticism that his heroes are all alike, that they are virtually the same man to whom he has given different names, perhaps even that they are all Dick Francis himself. His next novel *Twice Shy* presented such critics with an interesting opportunity to test the hypothesis, and it may be that Francis was having a small joke at their expense while laying their suggestions firmly to rest. In *Twice Shy* he inflicted the same criminal menace upon two men, and demonstrated that their individual characteristics and personalities would lead them to react differently. If the contrasts are not sufficiently clear, it is no evidence that Francis relies upon a set formula for his heroes; it is simply that the two men are brothers, and to distinguish between them in every detail would be to display a marked lack of realism.

By 1981, when *Twice Shy* was published in London, readers had long accepted that the standard component of a Francis novel was a male protagonist writing in the first person; it had become accepted that he shared with the reader the innermost thoughts of his hero, together with all the physical and psychological pain that hero might be called upon to endure. The structural difference of *Twice Shy*, however, is that it is divided into two parts. The first is narrated by schoolmaster Jonathan Derry, the second by his younger brother William.

"I told the boys to stay quiet while I went to fetch my gun," says Jonathan, immediately commanding attention with the first sentence in the novel. But this is not the outbreak of some typical Francis mayhem; it is Jonathan, a progressive teacher of physics, about to engage the interest of thirty bored teenagers by demonstrating what happens scientifically when a rifle fires a bullet. The contentment of Jonathan with his work, irrespective of the stimulating way in which he carries it out, still leaves the reader with the notion that he is really something of a dull dog. He is not specially ambitious, and he is also weighed down by an exhausted relationship with his wife Sarah. After eight years of marriage, he feels, there is nothing left at home but a debilitating sense of resignation and tedium; their inability to have children has led to a sullen cohabitation rather than a tempestuous disunion.

At this stage of the story, younger brother William is described as a noisy and independent-minded teenager. His ambition to become a jockey meets with the disapproval of both Jonathan and Sarah, although in Sarah's case it is part of her general intolerance toward the lively William. For his part, William thinks of security as a dirty word and holds no brief for safe jobs and orderly patterns of life. The cold calm of Jonathan and Sarah's domestic life is nevertheless undisturbed by this brother for whom Jonathan has been left responsible, since he is at boarding school and spends his holidays on farms in pursuit of his passion for riding horses.

An interruption in Jonathan and Sarah's unappetizing and spiritless existence comes suddenly, from a totally unexpected quarter. Their friends Peter and Donna Keithly, a similarly childless couple, desperately need moral support. Donna is in a suicidal state, having stolen a baby and been charged by the police. Then Jonathan is catapulted into a mystery that has little to do with baby stealing. Peter Keithly has a problem preying on his mind into which Jonathan is unenthusiastically drawn. A computer specialist, he has produced some programs relating to the handicapping of horses at the request of a chance acquaintance. Now that the work has been completed, he is being threatened by thugs demanding the programs. Jonathan unwittingly carries with him Peter's programs on tapes, secreted in commercial music cassettes. Two days later, Peter Keithly is killed by an explosion while preparing his cabin cruiser for what was to be Donna's recuperative holiday.

At this point the reader begins to see signs of an awakening in Jonathan Derry's spirit, the emergence of a more vital man both physically and cerebrally. There is a need for him to react physically when the thugs turn their attention to him following Peter's death. Jonathan is a rifle shot of Olympic Games standard, although he eschews violence. He deters the thugs initially with firearms he has at hand, but promises to send the computer tapes to them. He is one of Francis's reluctant heroes, requiring even more than the pressures exerted upon his predecessors to be goaded into aggressive action.

Jonathan's preference is to keep the violence suspended, to trust that his promise of cooperation will hold the villains at bay. In the meantime he concentrates upon cerebral activity, much more his forte, and with the help of fellow schoolmaster Ted Pitts he plays the tapes and discovers that they contain a scientific system for picking race winners. Here is Francis again showing his skilled hand at a second string in his bow; in *Reflex* it is photography, in *Twice Shy* it is computers, but in both is seen Francis's ability to educate the nontechnical in enjoyable technicalities.

Ted Pitts is a nicely sketched character. Impecunious as a result of nothing more extravagant than having to stretch a teacher's salary to feed and clothe three small children and keep a ramshackle car on the road, he lives in a mobile home on a caravan site—conditions wryly described as "not calculated to impress some of the social-climbers in the P.T.A." Despite a shortage of life's minor luxuries, circumstances that place many a marriage under strain, the Pitts family is happy and loving. Any tendency towards sympathy on Jonathan's part is quickly seen by him to be misplaced, and instead the carefree atmosphere raises in Jonathan's mind the possibility that Ted might be luckier than he:

> Ted was pushing his tiniest girl carefully around on a
> sort of turntable, holding her close to him and laughing

with her. I wished quite surprisingly fiercely that I could
have had a child like that, that I could have taken her to a
sunny park on Sunday mornings, and hugged her little
body and watched her grow. Sarah, I thought. Sarah . . .
this is the way you've ached, perhaps; and for the baby to
cuddle, and the young woman to see married. This is the
loss. This, that Ted Pitts has. I watched his delight in the
child and I envied him with all my heart.[11]

The rest of Jonathan Derry's story is a battle of wills, with
a crooked father-and-son team determined to secure the computer tapes and Jonathan's newfound confidence forbidding
him to give them up. He has to use various crafty ploys, and to
call upon his skill with a rifle, before successfully concluding
his encounter with the criminals. The value of the tapes becomes clear to Jonathan as he learns of their history; from the
original creation of systematic racing data by a harmless and
trusting old man, through the theft of the system by the trickster who employed Peter Keithly to program the data for a
computer, and to the inexorable pursuit of the tapes by Harry
Gilbert and his son Angelo, a picture of treachery and murder
develops. The final crisis, and the confrontation between Jonathan Derry and the Gilberts, provides Jonathan's marriage
with its severest test and determines his future.

The Gilberts are reminiscent of the Riveras in *Bonecrack*, except that Francis reverses the roles by making the father indisposed to extreme physical violence and the son a
vicious and sadistic killer. A favorite Francis motif is nevertheless there, with father and son growing apart until there is
a complete breakdown of authority, with the father powerless
to keep control; in *Bonecrack* this breakdown is to the good,
in *Twice Shy* it is for ill.

The people with whom Jonathan comes into contact provide ample opportunities for Francis to present the intriguing
cameo portraits he does so well. In addition to Ted Pitts and
the Gilberts there is the octogenarian Mrs. O'Rorke, the

widow of the old man who first compiled the racing data. Francis introduces her with an affecting degree of respect:

> "One does not grow silly with age. If one was silly when young, one may be silly when old. If one were acute when young, why should acuteness wane?"
> "I have done you," I said slowly, "an injustice."
> "Everyone does," she said indifferently. "I look in my mirror. I see an old face. Wrinkles. Yellow skin. As society is now constituted, to present this appearance is to be thrust into a category. Old woman, therefore silly, troublesome, can be pushed around."[12]

Francis is also adept at altering our opinions of his characters as the stories progress. In spite of Sarah Derry's childlessness, it is difficult at first to sympathize with her sullen frigidity. As the story moves on, it becomes possible to understand her more clearly; and as humanity begins to show through, with Donna's problems enabling Sarah to put her own in perspective, the healing of her marriage becomes a very real and desirable aim shared by the reader.

The experiences narrated by Jonathan Derry form a story that is complete in itself, novella length and satisfactorily rounded. The second half of the book sees Jonathan's conflict with the Gilberts resurrected after fourteen years and transferred to his brother William, who assumes the role of narrator. By this time it is not the youthful William with his head in the clouds about a future in racing, but a William who has developed great strength of character and determination. He is an experienced racing man, with years spent in every aspect of the sport.

While William has the personality to make a virtue out of his job-hopping and his spirit of wanderlust, there are barren periods that need to be filled if only to eat. It is at one such point that William's narrative begins, with Jonathan still showing the reliable brotherly touch by providing him with an introduction that secures him a managerial job with a top owner of racehorses. In his new position of responsibility, with the task of buying and selling horses with millions of pounds at stake, William has every reason to feel satisfied. Living with his girlfriend in a cottage near Newmarket, found for them by the village publican who rejoices in the name of Bananas Frisby, William's circumstances are settled to an extent that he never believed he would find acceptable. His lot is certainly a good one when placed in the context of the horrific world described by his philosophical friend Bananas:

> He had no politics, no god, no urge to agitate. People, he said, were known to starve on rich fertile tropical earth; people stole their neighbors' lands; peoples murdered peoples from racial hate; peoples tortured and killed in the name of freedom. It sickened him, he said. It had been going on from prehistory, and it would go on until the vindictive ape was wiped out.[13]

The unacceptable face of the world is nearer to home than William realizes, and is soon to erupt into his own world. When Angelo Gilbert is finally let out of prison, he is looking for revenge and still seeking the computer tapes that could make his fortune. What he finds, in attacking the younger Derry, is a man far less reserved and undemonstrative than his former adversary. William is a man who will fight without giving quarter.

The theme of this second half of *Twice Shy* is that of contrasts. William sets out to solve his problems in a manner directly contrasting with that of his brother. He is determined to master the situation presented to him by Angelo's blatant attack, just as he has the power and strength to overcome the resentment displayed towards him by those over whom his new job has placed him. He faces a series of clashes, but, unlike Jonathan, he will fight back positively rather than display patience and guile.

The second contrast is in the fortunes of the Pitts family. The formerly impecunious Ted, now no longer a schoolmaster, has grown rich from using a duplicate set of the computer tapes with which Jonathan rewarded him for his help fourteen years earlier. Thirdly there is the change in Angelo Gilbert, not so much a contrast as a degeneration; from the brutish youngster of Jonathan's story, he has changed into a hardened man, a psychopath, a paranoiac.

It has already been said that Jonathan's story is complete in itself, yet William's story proves to be essential in order to round out an account of one man's descent. That man is Angelo Gilbert. While Francis has much to tell us about the Derry brothers, in a strange way the complete book is the story of Angelo. Its shattering climax is calculated to touch even the most unemotional reader.

9

The Hero as Financier
and Kidnap Consultant
Banker
The Danger

"There are some folk," wrote Eric Hiscock, "who insist that Dick Francis's greatest achievement was winning (and, alas, losing) Aintree's Grand National on the Queen Mother's horse, Devon Loch. . . . It was not to be the ex-jockey's greatest achievement, however: that is his new novel, *Banker*."[1] One year later, with equal certainty that Dick Francis had gone from strength to strength, Hiscock described *The Danger* as "the most unputdownable thriller I have ever read, and that includes everything by Ian Fleming, and *The Day of the Jackal*."[2]

The simple fact is that Dick Francis has produced his finest books most recently, and has reached a pinnacle. He has developed beyond measure. His plotting ability and his mastery of suspense have increased with the years, but what has become manifest is his interest in people and in human relationships. His most recent novels spend more time upon this than most of his early works, his exploration of character

131

and the many influences upon the psyche being more evident aspects of the work he has produced since his growth into a fine writer with something to say. This is no belittlement of the straightforward thriller or adventure novelist, but merely a recognition that a few bring something to their craft that sets them apart from the crowd. Dick Francis is one of them.

Banker continues his tradition of employing a male narrator, a tradition that is unlikely to be broken in the future. On this occasion it is Tim Ekaterin, employed by the merchant bank in London founded by his great-grandfather. The pressures on Tim are considerable, and he is seen grappling with personal and emotional problems to which a less honorable man would succumb by taking the line of least resistance. In love with Judith, the young wife of his boss Gordon Michaels, he suffers in silence and will not yield to the temptation of an extramarital affair because of his respect for Gordon. His professional dilemma is no less acute: possessing genuine business flair, he knows that his promotion has come to him by birthright but is determined to prove his ability, while his rivals and an older director watch constantly for him to make bad decisions and misjudgments.

Gordon Michaels is a tragic figure. Judith and Tim are on the brink of an amorous relationship, but Gordon is unaware that their affection for him is forestalling it. Gordon is also a dying man, suffering from Parkinson's disease and relying upon prescribed drugs that cause hallucinations. *Banker* opens with some poignant scenes as Gordon reaches the breaking point, imagining that he is being pursued by white-faced clowns and that his only escape is by immersion in water.

> He looked pathetic in his red blanket, the sharp mind confused with dreams, the well-groomed businessman a pre-fountain memory, the patina stripped away. This was the warrior who dealt confidently every day in millions,

this huddled mass of delusions going home in wet trou-
sers. The dignity of man was everywhere tissue-paper
thin.[3]

It is at least possible for Tim to conceal his repressed feelings for Judith by absorbing himself in his work; spurred on
by the recollection that he unwillingly entered the business
following his father's death and his mother's bankruptcy, he
has been surprised to discover that he has a feel for the work
coupled with a resolute intention to prove himself.

> I suppose it was in my blood. All the snooty teenage scorn
> I'd felt for "money-grubbing," all the supercilious dis-
> approval of my student days, all the negative attitudes
> bequeathed by my failure of a father, all had melted
> into comprehension, interest and finally delight. The art
> of money management now held me as addicted as any
> junkie, and my working life was as fulfilling as any
> mortal could expect.[4]

In fact Francis not only presents a clear and fascinating
picture of the operation of a merchant bank, but through Tim
he demonstrates the virtues and social qualities of capitalism
by showing the human face of the money market. The technical workings of the Paul Ekaterin merchant bank are conveyed in his usual instructive, painstakingly researched yet
entertaining manner. More striking, however, are the engag-
ing subplots that illustrate how money can be made to work
for ordinary people with vision, providing that there are those
like Tim with faith and a willingness to persuade more cau-
tious superiors to take an occasional risk. Francis also shows
that the profits made by financiers cannot be legitimately
criticized when one considers that they suffer the vulnerability of all gamblers, a point he makes in his customarily laconic
style:

The gambles were all long term. You cast your bread
on the waters and hoped it would float back in the future
with butter and jam.
Mildew . . . too bad.[5]

Tim's principal gamble provides the main plot—bringing the
world of merchant banking into contact with the more familiar
Francis world of horse racing.

At first sight it is strange that Tim should eagerly accept
an invitation to join a party sharing a box at Ascot, since his father drank himself into a heart attack on the racing scene and
his mother gambled away the family capital. Yet Tim is philosophical about the sport that throughout his childhood was a
way of life. He recalls how his parents had enjoyed themselves, and ruefully asks himself who could say it was a fortune ill spent. This chance visit to Ascot provides the starting
point for a plot that is as exciting and scientifically ingenious
as anything Francis has produced. There are also elements of
violence and suspense that do not rely upon physical combat
between the narrator and assorted heavies—the kind that
Francis has described so competently in earlier books—but
stem from quite another source. In *Banker* it is not principally
a human being who is at risk; it is a business—and a racehorse. Again, although two murders are committed in the
course of the book, the outright thuggery of some other
Francis novels is replaced by a calculated deception that is all
the more chilling for its scientific precision.

The focal point of the mystery—in many respects the
central character, despite the fact that the action is seen
through Tim Ekaterin's eyes—is a stallion called Sandcastle.
A clear winner when Tim and his colleagues visit Ascot,
Sandcastle is purchased by breeder Oliver Knowles after Tim
places his career on the line by persuading his board to lend
five million pounds. There is no doubt in his mind that the
champion's progeny will justify the substantial stud fees
Knowles is anticipating, nor that the results will put the

Knowles stud farm securely on the map and provide a cast-iron investment for the Ekaterin merchant bank. It is nevertheless a highly unusual venture, one the more traditional directors see as an untenable risk.

Tim's business relationship with Oliver Knowles develops into a close personal friendship. Francis is able to show the growth in Tim's concern for Knowles and his domestic situation—his wife has left him to bring up a teenage daughter—because the time span of the story enables him to do so with complete credibility. Soon, when all begins to turn sour, Tim's position as financier and guardian of his bank's interests changes into that of father-confessor to young Ginnie Knowles and supporter of Oliver Knowles.

The blow eventually befalling Knowles is that a high proportion of Sandcastle's foals are born with serious deformities. Now Francis brings out the humanitarian in Tim, as well as the detective who lurks within all his hero narrators. Sandcastle's value and the future of the stud farm will be irreparably damaged, unless it can be proved that there is no defect in Sandcastle himself. Tim sets out to seek proof to save Knowles from bankruptcy, motivated more by his personal feelings than by pressure from his bank to maximize their return. The bond between Tim and Oliver Knowles becomes even stronger when Ginnie is the victim of an apparently motiveless murder that, together with the earlier murder of a vet, convinces Tim that he is faced with a criminal plot by someone who is prepared to kill to avoid exposure.

There are three skillfully interwoven themes in *Banker*. In addition to finance and horse-breeding, pharmacy plays a significant role. The identification of the method used to spoil Sandcastle's progeny is a fascinating and totally credible process, revealing a villain with a scientific technique that is infinitely more frightening than the bully-boy tactics of earlier Francis criminals. While the hero does not completely escape physical attack—this time not by thugs but by confinement with a berserk drugged horse—the violence in *Banker* stems from the cold and deliberate manipulation of nature itself.

The relationships developed by the narrator are always an important aspect of Francis's work, and one to which he gives painstaking attention. In *Banker* he provides evidence of his maturity as a novelist by probing more deeply than in most earlier novels and by exploring the feelings of Tim Ekaterin towards a whole range of characters. The most important relationships, calculated to reveal most about Tim himself, are with Ginnie Knowles and Judith Michaels. Judith regards Tim as "a man without sorrows, unacquainted with grief," while still recognizing the torment of their secret and undemonstrative love for each other:

> "Why do we *care*?" she said explosively. "Why don't we just get into your bed and have a happy time? Why is the whole thing so tangled up with bloody concepts like honor?" . . .
> We went indoors in a sort of deprived companionship, and I realized only when I saw Gordon's smiling unsuspicious face that I couldn't have returned there if it had been in any other way.[6]

Fifteen-year-old Ginnie is loved by Tim in quite another sense, and he becomes the father figure who understands her adolescent insecurity more clearly than the father who is beset with marital and business problems. Later Tim's pain is acute when Ginnie witnesses the birth of a deformed foal, and finally his anguish turns to grief at her murder:

> I'd thought of her young life once as being a clear stretch of sand waiting for footprints, and now there would be none, now only a blank, chopping end to all she could have been and done, to all the bright love she had scattered around her.
> "Oh . . . *Ginnie*," I said aloud, calling to her hopelessly in tearing body-shaking grief. "Ginnie . . . little Ginnie . . . come back."

But she was gone from there. My voice fled away into
darkness, and there was no answer.[7]

Banker is a beautifully handled fusion of love story and
mystery, together with its many specialist ingredients. The
whole is a cogent explanation of Dick Francis's phenomenal
popularity, showing his rare ability as a communicator, an ed-
ucator without pedantry, a thinker without partiality. To describe it simply as a thriller would be to ignore its many other
qualities, and to read it simply to be thrilled would be to de-
prive oneself of the other emotions it invokes.

While *Banker* is the proof positive that might lead critics
to make the patronizing assertion that Francis has become a
genuine novelist rather than a storyteller, *The Danger* may be
described as an international thriller of the highest quality.
Banker is arguably his most complex work, in its exploration
of themes and relationships within and without the main story
line; whether or not he chooses to take this line further in the
future, it is no adverse criticism of *The Danger* to suggest that
on this occasion he has not done so. Instead he reaches new
heights of suspense as he examines the age-old yet contemporary menace of kidnapping from an original angle.

Andrew Douglas, the narrator, has a job that shocks
with the implication of its necessity. He works for a firm
called Liberty Market Ltd., the business of which is to give
advice to potential kidnap victims and to minimize the danger
to actual victims by providing trained negotiators and investigators. Reviewing *The Danger*, T. J. Binyon expressed surprise that Francis had not previously adopted kidnapping as
the principal theme for one of his books, since imprisonment
or bondage had been one of his recurrent motifs.[8] While examples spring readily to mind of his heroes suffering such in-
dignities, and in some cases even the extended torture that
has led to accusations of sadism in his work—Rob Finn
(*Nerve*), Edward Lincoln (*Smokescreen*), Roland Britten
(*Risk*), Tim Ekaterin (*Banker*)—the theme is incidental to the

plot rather than the raison d'être. There are also many other instances, perhaps more interesting, where his hero suffers the different kind of imprisonment brought about by psychological influences or domestic circumstances.

Rob Finn is left to a slow death, soaked with freezing water and hung from a hook in an isolated tack room, because his psychotic enemy's insane jealousy has finally gone over the edge into murder; it is the climax of the story, not the story itself, and it has the effect of motivating Rob to retaliate in kind. Edward Lincoln's bondage in the heat of Africa is again a murder attempt, and serves also as an ironical replay of the scene in his latest "super-hero" movie—James Bondage, no less. While Roland Britten spends a large part of *Risk* imprisoned by unknown adversaries, it is simply a means to an end, a temporary deprivation of liberty intended to prevent him from carrying out his financial investigations. Tim Ekaterin's close confinement with a berserk stallion, though terrifying in itself, is but the equivalent of the scene of penultimate reckoning found in many other books when the villain has been unmasked by the hero and attempts unsuccessfully to silence him.

What gives *The Danger* its distinction is that the theme of kidnapping is dominant. Francis seizes the opportunity to explore this most violent and terrible of crimes, provoking and troubling his readers into considering its effects upon the victim and the victim's domestic circle. It is also an examination of the mind and motivation of the kidnapper, showing the simplism of assuming that the perpetrators are necessarily stereotyped thugs prompted by financial greed alone. The thesis is that there exists a need to understand the psychology of this area of crime, and to understand it in relation to those on both sides of the law; such knowledge can then be applied in order to avert bloodshed, or indeed a bloodbath, and this fully justifies the existence of an organization like Liberty Market and an operative like Andrew Douglas.

The Danger is a truly international story, its three sections set in Italy, England, and the USA. A kidnapping has already taken place before the novel opens; the victim, girl jockey Alessia Cenci, is in danger because the carabinieri have moved in as the ransom is about to be paid. "There was a God-awful cock-up in Bologna," says Andrew Douglas crisply in the first paragraph, and he is left with the job of retrieving the situation so that Alessia can be returned safely to her rich father Paolo.

How Andrew sets about bringing this particular kidnapping to a satisfactory conclusion, retaining Paolo's trust after a police blunder that could have resulted in Alessia's death, makes for enthralling reading. It stands up well if viewed as a craftsmanlike tale by a master of suspense, but Francis makes it so much more. He establishes at the outset that Andrew's occupation depends for its success upon a cultivated rapport with the families of victims and an appreciation of the long-term stresses on the victims themselves, rather than merely the ability to outwit the criminal. Andrew defines all this concisely, recognizing the demands it has made upon him and the marks it has left:

> My relationship with victims' families was something like that of a doctor: called in in an emergency, consulted in a frightening and unsettling situation, looked to for miracles, leant on for succor. I'd set off on my first solo advisory job without any clear idea of the iron I would need to grow in my own core, and still after four years could quake before the demands made on my strength. Never get emotionally involved, I'd been told over and over during my training, you'll crack up if you do.
> I was thirty. I felt, at times, a hundred.[9]

In cases of kidnapping, as Andrew has discovered, the danger remains long after the kidnap itself has been successfully resolved. The paid-for victim can remain a victim, a prisoner of the psychological pressures inflicted during incarceration. So too can they become the victim of their newly impoverished family's despair and resentment, with the burden of guilt so transferred to the innocent.

In the Cenci family Andrew finds all the signs he has come to recognize. There is Alessia's sister, resentful of her own dependence upon her rich father and the fact that payment of an enormous ransom will reduce their luxurious existence to modest comfort. She also uses Alessia's kidnapping to fan her jealousy, commenting that "there wouldn't be the same agonized fuss over me." Paolo Cenci's reactions are more predictable, his grief and torment well conveyed to the reader as he first becomes secretive about the kidnapper's instructions, then frantic as he is sent to a succession of dummy collection points, and finally crushed as he parts with his fortune but still awaits the return of his daughter.

After Alessia's release, Andrew sees in her a sense of guilt for having been taken. He also sees a mind trying to cope with the contrasts between the humiliating conditions in which she has been kept, and her normal surroundings with all the comforts and trappings of wealth. Paolo is beleaguered by new thoughts that call for Andrew's help and support even though the kidnapping itself is over. Depressed by the fact that he has to sell the house so loved by his late wife, he is solaced by Andrew's logical response that she would have wished it because she loved Alessia too.

Andrew's return to England accompanied by Alessia, who plans to recuperate at the home of a widowed friend, marks something of an interlude. It is not an insignificant part of the book, however, as it explores Alessia's very gradual ascent from the depths in which her experience has left her. Andrew feels a growing attraction for her, coupled with a continuing desire to help her escape from the persistent emotional effects of her ordeal. She has become introverted, tearful, and has lost the will to ride. Through Andrew, Francis likens her state of mind to that of the prisoners returning from Vietnam—not joyful at their release, but broken down by the humiliation and deprivation of their imprisonment, and suffering in Andrew's words "the hurricane's path across the spirit."

The tender and revealing interlude is interrupted when Andrew is plunged into another kidnapping case. This time it is three-year-old Dominic Nerrity, whose parents are the owners of a Derby winner, and Andrew believes the horse-racing connection to be more than a coincidence. Again Francis shows the inside domestic story of the kidnapping and its human aspects, with the young mother heartlessly blamed by her husband for losing the child. The menace and the grief are no less stark, silhouetted against the background of an English seaside resort than the streets of Bologna. It is a self-contained story, like the Bologna case, but leaving the same loose ends in the emotional wreckage of the family assaulted by the crime. A strange consolation in all the anguish is that Alessia, viewing from the outside the effect upon the Nerritys, is able to come to terms with her own problems and regain her inner strength.

There is now little doubt that a resourceful villain, known in Italy as Giuseppe and in England as Peter, is specializing in kidnapping on the international racing scene and could have inside sources of information that identify lucrative possibilities. This racing connection is confirmed when the Senior Steward of the Jockey Club is snatched while visiting Washington, and Andrew is again called in. The final section of the book sees Andrew at first tracking down the kidnapper, and then facing danger himself as the kidnapper retaliates.

Each section of *The Danger* has its own meticulous buildup of suspense, but the linking feature is a cumulative battle of wills between two men who are unknown to each other. Giuseppe-Peter is an enigma, towards whom his victims express no hatred; the danger stems as much from the psychological effects of kidnapping as from the physical threat to the individual victim. It is ironic and thought-provoking, when Francis gives us such a clear understanding of the lasting damage inflicted upon innocent people by the criminal, to see Andrew opposing Giuseppe-Peter with single-mindedness but without malice, and at the conclusion almost with regret.

10

Winner's Enclosure

On both sides of the Atlantic, eminent critics have identified qualities in Dick Francis that they have apparently failed to find in many other popular novelists. Indeed it is normally the case that best-selling authors receive little recognition of their artistic and literary abilities, making it necessary to examine the reasons why Francis has been so favorably treated. What are, to use T. J. Binyon's phrase, the "Franciscan virtues"?[1]

Francis would succeed purely as a writer of thrillers. He can produce a plot that enthralls, often with violence that shocks. Then, however, he raises himself above the basic level by showing his willingness to think about the characters themselves rather than simply about what happens to them. Action and incident is important, but Francis is a percipient writer interested equally in human relationships, in why his characters behave in certain ways, and in what has made them the people they are. Dudley Doust's clever pun, "Francis is meticulous with his malice and forethought,"[2] recognizes Francis's ability to present a world in which extreme criminal aggressors and ordinary human beings with problems of their own share the same stage, and come into explosive conflict.

He does so with a rare combination of toughness (normally expected of a thriller writer) and compassion (normally not). He thus embodies some of the qualities of Raymond Chandler and Ian Fleming, but displays a complete lack of pretentiousness and is blessedly free of Fleming's somewhat irritating trendiness. Philip Larkin, who clearly held the work of Francis in high esteem, once referred to his books as "laconically gripping, and graphic in a way that eschews Chandler's baroque images and Fleming's colour-supplement brand names."[3]

Francis is a shrewd judge of character, a skilled observer of attitudes and personal traits. The people in his books are never cardboard figures, but are always living beings. He achieves this not by copious physical descriptions, but by using a character's actions and words to build a picture in the reader's mind. In this way he ensures that the movement of the story is not interrupted, and that the creation of suspense is not sacrificed. While some of the incidents and plot ideas may be larger than life, the reader develops an understanding of the participants by seeing their reaction to events and the part they play in them. It is important to Francis that he should present real people, although the circumstances in which they find themselves might be unusual. "Most of my characters," he says, "are a mixture of people I have known. Sometimes I get too close for comfort, and friends have chided me when they feel they have recognized someone. But the schemes and fiddles with which some of my characters become involved are intended only to be a fictional development of what is possible."[4]

Francis's exploration of character and human motivation is, of course, to be seen most clearly in his protagonists. Twenty-two such men have been seen in the earlier analyses of the novels, and in virtually all cases have been the reluctant hero, the man who finds himself unwittingly involved in mayhem, the recipient of the unwelcome attentions of the aggressor, culminating in the urge to retaliate in self-defense or to protect others. Sid Halley (*Odds Against, Whip Hand*), Gene Hawkins (*Blood Sport*), David Cleveland (*Slayride*), and Andrew Douglas (*The Danger*) are professional investigators, and as such cannot be described as ordinary men who become enmeshed against their will in violent circumstances, but in other respects they share the trials and tribulations of their fellow narrators. To varying extents all Francis protagonists have crosses to bear, which is a phrase frequently used by Francis himself, and most come sooner or later to the crunch point when their self-reliance is tested and they must overcome their worst fears. All are men of honor, gentlemen of integrity whose demeanor and performance in the face of adversity easily attract descriptions such as tenacious, stoic, and laconic. "Every last one of them," observed Newgate Callendar, "is infused with British upper-class virtues,"[5] while John C. Carr avoids the class distinction and perceptively draws attention to "the elusive factor in any analysis of Francis's success . . . his heroes are metaphors for England."[6]

As the list of Francis protagonists has grown, so it has become more difficult to give a simple description of the typical Francis hero. On a superficial level in the early days, it might have been possible to categorize them as financially secure and cultured men with successful family backgrounds, but there have been cases where important points have been made about money problems (Matt Shore in *Rat Race*) and lowly antecedents (Kelly Hughes in *Enquiry*, and Sid Halley again). Then it has been suggested that the Francis hero is employed in or around the racing world, and indeed it was so at the beginning, but there have been a succession of heroes who know little about racing and have had to acquire the necessary knowledge in the course of their adventures—beginning with undercover agent Gene Hawkins (*Blood Sport*) and pilot Matt Shore (*Rat Race*), and most recently Jonathan Derry (*Twice Shy*), Tim Ekaterin (*Banker*), and Andrew

Douglas (*The Danger*). Some critics have erroneously insisted upon stereotyping Francis heroes as racing people, whereas Francis himself has been at pains to introduce many variations. Moreover he has significant reasons for doing so, rather than merely to differentiate one from another. The specific expertise of each Francis hero is important in itself, relevant to the plot and to the decisions he has to make. Edward Lincoln in *Smokescreen* has his image as a movie hero severely tested; in *High Stakes*, Steven Scott's complex scheme to outwit the villains is compared to his ingenuity as a toymaker; Charles Todd (*In the Frame*) finds his knowledge of art vital and his ignorance of racing irrelevant; while in *Reflex*, Philip Nore's skill in photography is predominant.

Thus the typical protagonist cannot be defined by reference to social class, occupation, or involvement in the racing game. Are there, then, other features common to these heroes? The answer lies in two phrases already used: almost every one has a cross to bear and comes to a testing point in his life—these two factors being sometimes but not invariably related.

Heywood Hale Broun referred to Francis's "fondness for cripples—real, psychological or financial" and suggested that a positive reason for this was that "we root for the racer who starts three fences behind."[7] It is incontrovertible, however, that Francis uses this approach not simply to engage the reader's sympathy and support for his protagonist. "I like to explore a character's reactions to misfortune,"[8] says Francis, and it is normally the case that his hero's burdens and tragedies are genuinely relevant to the plot rather than an interesting complication. This applies whether the problems are large or small, and even small problems can have a disproportionate effect upon the life of someone following a particular occupation. Randall Drew in *Trial Run*, for example, suffers from astigmatism; not the most earth-shattering defect, one might think, until one appreciates that it has finished his career as a jockey, left him yearning for his past, and made the offer of a potentially exciting mission to Moscow more inviting because it could rescue him from a dull existence. David Cleveland (*Slayride*) is constantly made to feel inferior because of his comparative youth, which inspires him to show his worth as a Jockey Club investigator and pursue the villains in the face of the uncooperative Norwegian racing authorities. These disadvantages might seem trivial in comparison with Sid Halley's hand, crippled and finally lost, but they are nonetheless significant to the characters within the context of their own stories. Francis has also explored the psychological impact upon some of his protagonists when their parents reject them or lack confidence in them (for example in *Nerve*, *Bonecrack*, and *Reflex*), which then becomes their motivating factor, their raison d'être. Then again he has taken negative, reclusive, or world-weary personalities (*Flying Finish*, *Blood Sport*, and *Rat Race*) and shown how at the testing time they react positively and begin to control their own destiny. Subtler variations of this are Edward Lincoln (*Smokescreen*), who has rejected his public image as a tough movie star but is forced by circumstances to play this role in real life; and kidnap expert Andrew Douglas (*The Danger*), who has seen so much of human misery that he can find humor disconcerting. Finally, there are those whose pain is suffered at second hand: Ty Tyrone (*Forfeit*), whose disabled wife is both a target for the villains and a victim of his own infidelity; Kelly Hughes (*Enquiry*), who is given the strength to endure and to right a miscarriage of justice because he has already suffered the greater tragedy of his young wife's death; and Jonah Dereham (*Knockdown*), shouldering the onerous responsibility of an alcoholic brother.

These are not mere story devices, but evidence of Francis's commitment to thoughtful characterization. The crosses they bear, whether physical or emotional, give depth and feeling to his protagonists. They make of them genuine people, ordinary men rather than superheroes, and invite the reader to decide how he would behave in similar circumstances. The responses of these men, whatever criminal threat faces them, are often conditioned by their other problems. If they can conquer their private agonies and bring themselves back from the brink of despair, they can face the potential and actual violence of the criminals with newfound strength and confidence. This recurrent quality of his protagonists shows Francis to be a writer of perception, a sagacious judge of human beings; it was recognized at an early stage by C. P. Snow, who regarded it as Francis's greatest merit. "He has a most unusual psychological skill," said Snow. "Looking at a man (he looks with acute observation, and like all good novelists knows that the psyche and soma are one) he can guess what he may be able to do. . . . This sense of the possible future, of human potential and fatality, of the limits of energy, has almost departed from modern fiction: and yet a great part of personal judgment depends upon it."[9]

While the Francis hero can on occasions display the world-weariness and cynical humor of a hard-boiled private eye, and indeed has more than a touch of Chandler's honorable man who must go down those "mean streets," his toughness is as spiritual as it is physical. Essential humanity shows through, often under extreme provocation. "They have to keep their base instincts under control," says Francis, "and this requires self-examination. There is always a moment when the hero has to be tested, a moment of anger when their better self comes out."[10] Even so, Francis does not deal with this situation predictably or consistently, but takes each case on its merits and shows his understanding of the man in question. Jonah Dereham (*Knockdown*), finally facing his adversary, conquers an almost irresistible urge to kill him; but Henry Grey (*Flying Finish*) has no such compunction.

All these features of the Francis hero are important and relevant to the plots. Often their romantic entanglements, by contrast, are not. In fact Francis does not always give his heroes a love life, although some have a small sexual adventure along the way that adds little to the books concerned. These passing sexual encounters are often irrelevant, and have the effect of disturbing the story line. The partners in such instances are not characters who become fully extended or assume the role of heroine. Francis does not even make a special feature of them as sex objects, in the Ian Fleming tradition.

Newgate Callendar described the Francis hero as "an Arthurian knight, more Lancelot than Galahad, for he is not prissy and enjoys sex so long as the ground rules are observed."[11] It was just such ground rules that pricked the conscience of Ty Tyrone (*Forfeit*), creating a touching emotional triangle and providing a powerful subplot that contributed to its being one of Francis's finest books.

There are instances where, in his treatment of women rather than of sex, one can detect what really interests Francis as a writer. He excels in those cases where he presents a female character who is not a token of an obligatory romantic interest, nor dominated by the male in pursuit of sexual gratification, but has something positive to contribute. He does not dwell on feminine youth and beauty for its own sake, but often sets out with deliberation to give his women identifiable and thought-provoking roles. Thus Gabriella (*Flying Finish*) is interesting because she supplies illicit contraceptives to Italian women, Ginnie and Judith (*Bunker*) provide tender and contrasting examples of love without sex, and Alessia (*The Danger*) enables us to examine the effects of kidnapping upon the victim. Francis will also present, without tokenism, women who are highly successful in what are traditionally regarded as men's occupations—trainers Annie Villars (*Rat Race*) and Popsy Teddington (*The Danger*), head stable lad Etty Craig (*Bonecrack*), and air traffic controller Sophie Randolph (*Knockdown*) come to mind. When he chooses to depict explicit sexuality—and one recalls only Kari (*Slay-ride*) and Miss Pinlock (*Risk*)—it performs the function of drawing to attention the problems and pressures felt by the women concerned. Finally, and of supreme importance, it must be mentioned that Francis shows great intelligence and compassion in his approach to women who are suffering physical or emotional blows; whether they are scarred, crippled, widowed, or childless, he communicates the painful reality of their situation. In all such cases—the positive woman, the liberated woman, the flawed and suffering woman—one sees his skill in characterization at its best, and can easily forgive those trivial diversions when one of his women serves only as a piece of light romantic dalliance for the hero.

The protagonists in some cases are involuntarily involved in questionable activities. Jockeys, for example, are sometimes obliged to cooperate in the fixing of races. In general they also have to repay the villains in their own coin, and as amateur detectives they are able to acquire information or effect retribution in ways outside the law. It is all in a good cause, however, and throughout they remain models of morality, humanitarianism, and honor. The Francis villains, in total contrast, are almost invariably rotten to the core. They rarely display redeeming features. Even in those cases where they clearly suffer from psychological disorders (for example Kemp-Lore in *Nerve* and Enso Rivera in *Bonecrack*), their cruel and atrocious acts mean that Francis declines to secure any sympathy for them. Most are affluent and charming, flamboyantly dressed and well-manicured, but are common thugs under their veneer of nouveau riche respectability. When the hero stands in their way, any semblance of finesse disappears. They then reveal their true characters, taking a sadistic delight either in inflicting punishment or in ordering hired bully-boys to do their bidding. There is thus a very simple distinction between good and evil, although Francis will frequently acknowledge that in the final analysis we are all members of the human race, by condemning his villains to a pathetic or tragic end that can invite a last-minute compassionate response on the part of the reader.

"Fear stalks through these books; not the fear of the weakling, but that of the strong, or perhaps once strong, man doubting his strength under stress."[12] This statement by John Welcome is perhaps a useful starting point in any consideration of Francis's principal themes. Recalling *Nerve* and *Whip Hand*, for example, it is specifically correct. Yet while fear is not really a recurrent Francis theme in itself, Welcome's few words serve as a good general definition that could easily cover several of Francis's important issues. The books are indeed about men who have their strength tested, sometimes physical strength but often strength of character. This is inextricably linked with the question of morality, and that is the predominant Francis theme. It is the old kind of morality displayed by his protagonists, not the convenient semimorality or lack of morality seen in so many thriller heroes; in this way they differ from most private eyes and secret agents, although their exploits might be in other respects similar. "I would say that my heroes are gentlemen," Francis confirms. "They will not normally do anything which isn't cricket, as the saying goes. They will not take unfair advantage of the situation, or of the women. I could never write a book where the central character is a baddie, because I would never expect him to do something I would not do myself."[13] This does not mean that everything for the hero always works out neatly, or that his virtue is rewarded by a perfectly satisfactory conclusion to the plot: he might still lose the woman he loves, or be left with an injury, or find himself back at first base with psychological problems making it painful to face the business of living.

Francis's novels have about them a moral correctness that means the villains never triumph in the end, but they can still leave the scars that give the lie to those critics who feel his stories always end in tidy perfection. As Geoffrey Stokes asserted, Francis "has managed to embrace the modern skepticism about things that always work out neatly without accepting a world in which nothing can."[14] The Francis hero might strive so assiduously to play by the rules blatantly broken by the Francis villain that he will sometimes appear too good to be true. Close examination reveals, however, that the hero behaves like any ordinary and honorable man, and it is Francis who subjects him to the fickle hand of fate. The good die, often young, and the heroes are frequently damaged. On balance, Francis's morality does not fool him into presenting an unreal world.

It might also be stated that all Francis's novels involve a conflict between good and evil, and that often the evil is in the form of a conspiracy. Francis is not primarily concerned with the one-to-one tournament between detective and master criminal, the central theme of so many espionage tales or whodunit puzzles. His unlikely hero is instead placed in a situation where organized men have woven a web into which he is drawn, and which he must gird himself up to demolish. Not being a James Bond figure, he encounters fear and self-doubts when he realizes that he is one ordinary man against a powerful group of conspirators, and such realization often takes a long time to dawn. The conspiracy is so complex that the hero needs time to appreciate the nature of the opposition, although the motive of the conspirators normally transpires as simple and age-old. "As surely as the spreading pool of intergenerational guilt characterises Ross Macdonald's work," commented Stokes, "the corrupting influence of money marks Francis's. Money and . . . class."[15]

Taking this latter point, one can also link with the question of class that of parental influence. It has provided Francis with one of his most powerful and frequently recurring themes —the search for identity. Often the hero is made to feel inferior or out of place by the villains, as is Sid Halley, but he is even more frequently treated in this way by members of his own family. Examples are numerous, but particularly prominent are the cases of Henry Grey (*Flying Finish*) and Kelly Hughes (*Enquiry*). Henry rejects his upper-class background and incurs his family's displeasure by seeking to live his own life, yet still atttacts the odium Billy Watkins reserves for the aristocracy. Kelly leaves behind his working-class background, and his parents despise him for successively obtaining higher education and becoming a jockey, yet they are revolted when his success as a jockey is shattered by the disqualification they imagine brings shame upon them. Fred Erisman has examined these two cases in particular, suggesting that "Francis's point in these two novels is the same. England in the 1960s is a world of social change, a world in which a title can be as much a liability as an asset, a world in which Bernard Shaw's fulminations about education and accent have proven to be true."[16] Francis's novels are full of people who have moved away from their familial roots, either gradually or in open rebellion, whether prompted by the autocracy of their fathers (never mothers) or merely by their need to stand or fall on their own initiative.

Always this is achieved with the gritty determination that is the hallmark of the typical Francis hero, who displays the compulsion to do his own thing just as Francis himself has done. Interestingly, because Francis has personally succeeded in disparate fields of endeavor, so too do his heroes prove that they can make their own way in the world by their very versatility—they can be jockey and pilot, antique dealer and trainer, toymaker and racehorse owner, accountant and jockey, photographer and jockey, and so on.

A further Francis theme, not entirely divorced from the question of morality mentioned earlier, is that identified by Michael N. Stanton. "Francis's fiction," he says, "is about learning to love . . . to be fully human. The satisfaction really

comes . . . through their adherence to a set of values: the
price of learning to need, the value of being vulnerable, the
inestimable worth of human love."[17] When we think of Matt
Shore's slow recovery from cold negativity (*Rat Race*) and
Neil Griffon's positive influence upon the young Alessandro
Rivera (*Bonecrack*), among many others, there can be no
doubt that Stanton has a valid point.

It is therefore easily established that Dick Francis is a
writer with something to say. He makes no claim to be a communicator of deep significance, and certainly would not suggest that his work is a vehicle by which political or social messages are conveyed, but it would satisfy him to know that his
themes and subplots, together with his characterization, are
recognized as displaying uncommon wisdom and compassion.
If he is seen to understand his fellow men, that is praise
enough. It must be borne in mind, however, that Francis is
primarily a writer of thrillers. In spite of their other excellent
qualities, his books will stand or fall when judged on the staple ingredients of the good thriller. These too must be considered, rather than being taken for granted.

His ability to devise an enthralling plot is not open to
question. Any debate on this point between critics, in the unlikely event that such a debate might occur, would be irrelevant. The fact that countless readers find his stories compulsive, and that he is one of the few authors writing today who
justify the clumsy compliment "unputdownable," is sufficient
evidence of his plotting flair. Similarly he is an acknowledged
master of pacing and suspense, knowing precisely when to
pile on the action and when to cut and fade, leaving the
reader during more contemplative or leisurely passages waiting on tenterhooks for the next explosive onslaught. When
the hero is in a tight corner, imprisoned or at the mercy of the
aggressors, the reader knows that he will eventually escape
but one pushes this knowledge to the back of the mind as

Francis builds up the agony with excruciating deliberation. His many chases, often cat-and-mouse pursuits with the tables turning unexpectedly, are brilliantly achieved. His climaxes, with the hero fighting for his life against the criminals or sometimes against the elements, are staple ingredients of the thriller that nobody does better than Francis. It has been frequently mentioned that his pacing expertise, his infallible instinct for the right moment to pull back or thrust his narrative forward, is derived from his steeplechasing experience, and Francis freely admits that it is probably the signal contribution made by his first career to his second.[18]

Francis's readability, and his talent for action and suspense, stem from his economical use of words. "Whatever I now know about writing," he says, "I learnt from the discipline of working for a newspaper. There was small space allowed so that every word had to be worth it, and a deadline to be met so it was no good turning in a masterpiece tomorrow."[19] He is no longer faced with the space constraints of a newspaper column, but still believes that every word must be worthwhile. "I use a punchy style, avoiding long descriptive passages, and keep it flowing. Many readers have told me that the economy of language and the resulting pace is what attracts them to my books."[20] H. R. F. Keating has applauded the fact that "Francis never succumbs to the temptation to use a long or complex word where a simple one exists, something that writers with high reputations are often guilty of."[21]

None of this must be taken to mean that the quality of Francis as a writer is in question. Clipped descriptions and punchy dialogue have been the stock in trade of some of the world's most acclaimed novelists, while nearer to Francis's field the effective deployment of few words has typified the best exponents of the thriller, particularly those of the hardboiled private-eye school. Indeed Raymond Chandler's tongue-in-cheek advice, "when in doubt have a man come through a door with a gun in his hand,"[22] is a technique of which Francis would approve. He has followed this dictum, literally or metaphorically, as in this example from *Forfeit*:

> Bought the cake. Came out into the street. Heard a voice in my ear. Felt a sharp prick through my coat abeam the first lumbar vertebra.
> "It's a knife, Mr. Tyrone." . . .
> I got in. There was a chauffeur driving, all black uniform and a stolid acne-scarred neck. The man with the knife climbed in after me and settled by my side. I glanced at him, knew I'd seen him somewhere before, didn't know where. I put *Tally* and the apple cake carefully on the floor. Sat back. Went for a ride.[23]

Francis's artistry lies in what he does with his few words. He makes them work, producing an apt comment upon life or death, or a cynicism of Chandleresque simplicity:

> "Dying is a relative term when it doesn't end in death."[24]

> "Self-analysis . . . did you study it?"
> "No. Lived it. Like everyone does."[25]

> "This doesn't look like a killing matter, Sid."
> "You never know what is until you're dead."[26]

He has a marvelous eye for a neat or caustic metaphor that conveys perfect meaning. In *Blood Sport*, the atmosphere in an old hired car is "as fresh as last week's news and as hot as tomorrow's,"[27] while in *Slayride* the air of Norwegian businessmen is "the rat race taken at a walk. Very civilized."[28] In *Knockdown* a horse "ambled over with all the urgency of a museum,"[29] and a criminal faced with exposure "gave a great imitation of Lot's wife."[30] Simon Searle in *Flying Finish* "flowed down from the stool like a green corduroy amoeba,"[31] while the rich but sickly Randall Drew in *Trial Run* describes his birthright as "a silver spoon that bent easily."[32]

Such examples serve to give the flavor of Francis's one-liners, although he can be equally effective at slightly greater length. When actor Edward Lincoln visits South Africa in *Smokescreen* and is quizzed about his attitude to apartheid, he explains:

> "I belong to a profession . . . which never discriminates against blacks or Jews or women or Catholics or Protestants or bug-eyed monsters, but only against non-members of Equity."[33]

In *Slayride* there is this description of a Norwegian, formerly a World War II resistance leader but now grown old:

> "He has solidified into a dull lump, like the living core of a volcano pouring out and dying to dry gray pumice."[34]

In many instances Francis displays an ironical appreciation of incongruity, as when Tim Ekaterin (*Banker*) visits a cold and immaculate stud farm:

> There were no dead leaves as such to be seen. No flower beds, no ornamental hedges, no nearby trees. A barren mind, I thought, behind a business whose aim was fertility and the creation of life.[35]

It is frequently said that Francis is not a descriptive writer, nor a writer who imparts color. Yet all the requisite color and description is in his action, his dialogue, and his choice wordplay. This is most clearly to be observed in his scenes on and around the racetrack, which his own experience enables him to infuse with great feeling and detail. "His knowledge of the racing world creates a background of almost Dickensian realism for his stories,"[36] said Judith Rascoe, and specific reference has already been made to the Dotheboys parallel in *For Kicks*. Leaving Dickens aside, however, his communication to the reader of the atmosphere of the race-course in *Whip Hand* is but one of many examples in which he presents a complete picture concisely and effectively. He conveys the animated chatter outside the weighing room, the small talk and the critical conjecture about past races and races to come, the hard-luck stories, the nods and winks of the scandal-mongers.

> There were the scurrilous stories and the slight exaggera-tions and the downright lies. The same mingling of hon-our and corruption, of principle and expediency. People ready to bribe, people with the ready palm. Anguished little hopefuls and arrogant big guns. The failures making brave excuses, and the successful hiding the anxieties be-hind their eyes. All as it had been, and was, and would be, as long as racing lasted.[37]

No survey of Dick Francis's work can be complete with-out reference to his painstaking research, which makes such a major contribution to the authenticity of his plots and sub-plots. From a very early stage he ceased to rely completely upon his personal knowledge of the racing world, and recon-dite information on a variety of specialized fields has played an increasingly important part in his stories. From enticing mini-lectures, for example on the workings of a boiler and what makes it explode (*Odds Against*), he has developed to the stage where his second-string subject often virtually takes over the book (as does photography in *Reflex*, computers in *Twice Shy*, and wines and spirits in *Proof*). His desire to pre-sent a faultless exposition of such subjects, and to provide credible backgrounds to his stories, is indicated by the fact that he chooses not to write about places and things he has not experienced for himself. His overseas settings have evolved from visits made to the countries concerned, and his wife Mary Francis has become accomplished in such fields as painting, computers, and photography while researching for her husband's books. Her research into commercial aviation for *Flying Finish* led to flying lessons, and later to her establishing an air taxi business.[38] This in turn resulted in the novel *Rat Race*, and even to the writing of what has become a standard textbook on the subject.[39] All this is mentioned as evidence of the care with which the Francises, as a team, pay Dick Francis's readers the courtesy of providing them with a scrupulously prepared rather than hastily contrived product.

This assessment of the novels of Dick Francis has been an appreciation of the many qualities he brings to the art of writing thrillers, a recognition of the fact that he is among the contemporary élite of the field. It is unlikely that his books will be condemned to that capacious wastebasket that now contains the ephemeral works of so many of his predecessors, but instead there is every likelihood that his contribution to popular literature will be remembered in the future. It would nevertheless be wrong to ignore the fact that certain aspects of his work have occasionally been adversely criticized, and some mention of these points must be made here.

It is undeniable that Francis has sometimes been accused of the superfluous use of violence. Those who find this objectionable have normally gone further, and suggested that sadism has played too prominent a part in his stories. In chapter 3, when considering the injuries inflicted on Sid Halley by Howard Kraye, the point has already been made that this was entirely consistent with Kraye's character. Similar arguments could be used in respect of other examples of sadism in Francis's books, and it is reasonable to suggest that his credibility as a writer would suffer if he were to tone down such scenes merely because they might be found offensive. Offensiveness and undiluted evil are precisely the defects Francis intended to convey in the case of Kraye, and any criticism is ample evidence of Francis's success. It would also be unwise to take such violence out of context, since its effect upon the victim is one of Francis's most significant themes. In *Odds Against* it

provides a motivating force for Sid Halley, while the sequel
Whip Hand shows Sid in genuine fear of a sadistic repetition
at the hands of his new enemy. A further example, in *Flying
Finish*, serves to show that Billy Watkins is not merely the
disadvantaged youngster some sympathetic readers might assume, but a coldly cruel and vicious thug who deserves whatever Henry Grey metes out to him.

On violence in general, it could be contended that Francis introduces it sparingly. One must agree with the assessment of Julian Symons that "he has learned the thriller writer's lesson that violence is more effective when it is firmly
rationed";[40] when one considers the numerous beatings and
shootings inflicted by the villains (and indeed heroes) in the
works of so many other popular writers, criticism of Dick
Francis would appear misplaced. Bearing in mind the reaction to violence of his heroes, one also senses that Francis
has a more positive point to make than those writers who pan-
der to their readers' base passions. "Given the nature of the
hero," as Michael N. Stanton identified, "the violence is self-
defeating."[41]

Related to this question of violence, the statement is also
sometimes made that Francis's heroes take considerable punishment but bounce back unrealistically without displaying ill
effects. If there is some justification for this comment, it is a
failing that Francis shares with most others in the make-
believe world of the action thriller. Two points, however,
must be made in Francis's defense. First, he spent some years
in a sport that gave him an accurate idea of the limits of human physical endurance. He knows the capacity of a fit and
resilient man, and has his own personal record of injury and
recovery to prove it. Second, many of his protagonists have
been toughened in this sport that Francis knows so well. It is
strange that the words of Rob Finn, only the second hero
Francis created, did not disarm some of his critics:

> I was of course quite used to being knocked about. I
> followed, after all, an occupation in which physical dam-
> age was a fairly frequent though unimportant factor. . . .
> I had broken several of the smaller bones, been kicked in
> tender places, and dislocated one or two joints. . . . It
> seemed that in common with most other jockeys I had
> been born with the sort of resilient constitution that could
> take a bang and be ready for business, if not the following
> day, at least a good deal quicker than the medical profes-
> sion considered normal.[42]

The matter of his indestructible heroes is cited by some
critics who question Francis's credibility. There have been
others who have suggested that his plots themselves, and particularly the criminal schemes, are unrealistic. While this
could be adequately countered by reminding detractors that
Francis claims to be no more than a writer of fiction, he has
actually taken the argument further in an article of his own.
Referring to press notices describing his books as "far-
fetched," "straining the imagination," and "basically improb-
able," he cites two instances questioned by his New York
publisher: the hijack in *Flying Finish*, and the botched kidnapping in *Bonecrack*. Publication of these two books coin-
cided, respectively, with the very first aircraft hijack (from the
USA to Cuba) and the bungled kidnapping and murder of
Mrs. Muriel McKay in England. "If some outlandish bit of
plot has never actually occurred," Francis concludes, "the
reader's internal belief-computer may tell him it *cannot*. If
the fictional events have happened often the belief is easy,
but the book is boring. . . . I should rather be reviewed as 'im-
plausible' than 'predictable.'"[43]

Lest such niggling criticisms of Dick Francis be taken too
seriously, however, it is necessary to reiterate the point that
his work has been universally applauded. One has only to
consider the credentials of some of the Francis enthusiasts to
appreciate his significance as a popular novelist. Edmund

Crispin, creator of some of the most distinguished and intellectual detective stories of the twentieth century, described
him as "a beautiful writer, one of the few best-sellers who
never resorts for his appeal to banality or to clichés."[44] C. P.
Snow, referring to Francis's ability to judge the capacity and
human potential of his protagonists, considered that "it raises
his books a class above nearly anything of their kind. It gives
them their dynamic, their flux of internal energy, and . . .
their reassuring certainty that one is in the company of a wise
and grown-up man."[45] Finally Philip Larkin discouraged
those who would detract from Francis's literary ability simply
because he chooses to work in the thriller genre: "The temptation for Francis to become 'a real novelist' must be very
strong. Let us hope he resists it; he is always twenty times
more readable than the average Booker entry."[46]

It will have become obvious that the author of this volume shares the opinions of these eminent commentators, and
the many others who feel that Dick Francis has made an outstanding contribution to popular literature. He is a writer who
warrants such recognition.

Notes

Form Book

1. Heywood Hale Broun, "Dick Francis and the Racing Game," *The Washington Post Book World* (27 March 1983). Review of *Banker*.

2. Julian Symons, Review of *Reflex*, *The New York Times Book Review* (29 March 1981), 3, 45.

3. Author's interview with Dick Francis, London, 14 September 1983.

4. Timothy Foote, "Reading and Riding," *Time* magazine (22 May 1972). Review of *Bonecrack*.

5. Alistair Burnet, "Straight from the Horse's Mouth," *The Listener* 92 (22 August 1974), 235–237.

6. C. P. Snow, "Over the Sticks," *Financial Times* (19 July 1973), 33.

7. Philip Larkin, Review of *Banker*, *The Observer* (17 October 1982).

8. Jessica Mann, "The Suspense Novel," in *Whodunit? A Guide to Crime, Suspense and Spy Fiction*, edited by H. R. F. Keating (London: Windward, 1982; New York: Van Nostrand Reinhold, 1982), 60.

9. Michael N. Stanton, "Dick Francis: The Worth of Human Love," *The Armchair Detective* 15, #2 (1982), 137–143.

10. Edward Zuckerman, "The Winning Form of Dick Francis," *The New York Times Magazine* (25 March 1984), 40 ff.

163

11. Author's interview.

12. Dick Francis, *The Sport of Queens*, Third revised edition (London: Michael Joseph, 1982), 243–244.

13. Author's interview.

14. Zuckerman, "The Winning Form of Dick Francis."

15. Michael M. Thomas, "Francis on Track with Latest Thriller," *The Philadelphia Inquirer* (27 March 1983). Review of *Banker*.

16. John Mortimer, "Don't Give me Shakespeare! Interviews with Dick Francis and Catherine Cookson," *Sunday Times* (15 August 1982), 25. Also in *In Character*, by John Mortimer (London: Allen Lane, 1983).

17. Raymond Chandler, letter to James Sandoe, 16 June 1949. In *Raymond Chandler Speaking*, edited by Dorothy Gardiner and Kathrine Sorley Walker (Boston: Houghton Mifflin, 1962; London: Hamish Hamilton, 1962).

18. John Leonard, Review of *Reflex*, *The New York Times* (20 March 1981), 21.

19. Snow, "Over the Sticks."

1. The Hero as Himself

1. Dick Francis, *The Sport of Queens: The Autobiography of Dick Francis* (London: Michael Joseph, 1957; New York: Harper & Row, 1969). This book is now in its third revised edition (London: Michael Joseph, 1982) but no revision has appeared in the USA to date. Page references throughout these notes relate to the US edition, unless otherwise specified.

2. Francis, *The Sport of Queens*, 16.

3. Ibid., 42.

4. Ibid., 82.

5. Ibid., 226.

6. Ibid., 223.

7. Dick Francis, *Forfeit* (New York: Harper & Row, 1969), 151.

8. Francis, *The Sport of Queens*, Third revised edition, 247.

9. Author's interview with Dick Francis, London, 14 September 1983.

2. The Hero as Jockey, Hate Object, and Spy
Dead Cert, Nerve, For Kicks

1. Dick Francis, *Dead Cert* (New York: Holt Rinehart, 1962), 5. All page references throughout these notes relate to this edition.
2. Ibid., 13.
3. Ibid., 36.
4. Ibid., 58.
5. Ibid., 9.
6. Ibid., 28–9.
7. Ibid., 75.
8. Ibid., 39–40.
9. Ibid., 94.
10. Ibid., 95–96.
11. Author's interview with Dick Francis, London, 14 September 1983.
12. Francis, *Dead Cert*, 127.
13. Ibid., 128.
14. Ibid., 165.
15. Anthony Boucher, Review of *Nerve*, *The New York Times Book Review* (5 April 1964), 48.
16. Dick Francis, *Nerve* (New York: Harper & Row, 1964), 1. All page references throughout these notes relate to this edition.
17. Ibid., 7.
18. Ibid., 11–12.
19. Ibid., 22.
20. Ibid., 64.
21. Ibid., 127.
22. Dick Francis, *For Kicks* (New York: Harper & Row, 1965), 12–13. All page references throughout these notes relate to this edition.
23. Ibid., 13.
24. Ibid., 114.
25. Ibid., 132–135.
26. Anthony Boucher, "Criminals at Large," *The New York Times Book Review* (21 March 1965), 22. Review of *For Kicks*.

27. Snow, "Over the Sticks."

3. The Hero as Halley *Odds Against, Whip Hand*

1. Dick Francis, *Odds Against* (New York: Harper & Row, 1966), 57. All page references throughout these notes relate to this edition.
2. Ibid., 63.
3. Author's interview with Dick Francis, London, 14 September 1983.
4. Francis, *Odds Against*, 142.
5. Ibid., 112.
6. Ibid., 245–246.
7. John C. Carr, "Dick Francis," in *The Craft of Crime: Conversations with Crime Writers*, by John C. Carr (Boston: Houghton Mifflin, 1983), 222.
8. Francis, *Odds Against*, 249.
9. Ibid., 267–268.
10. Author's interview.
11. Francis, *The Sport of Queens*, Third revised edition, 243.
12. Dick Francis, *Whip Hand* (New York: Harper & Row, 1980), 2. All page references throughout these notes relate to this edition.
13. Ibid., 15.
14. Ibid., 43.
15. Ibid.
16. Ibid., 44.
17. Ibid., 67.
18. Ibid., 105, 123.
19. Carr, "Dick Francis," 205.
20. Francis, *Whip Hand*, 293.

4. The Hero as Reluctant Peer, Weary Agent, and Newspaperman *Flying Finish, Blood Sport, Forfeit*

1. Dick Francis, *Flying Finish* (New York: Harper & Row, 1967), 6. All page references throughout these notes relate to this edition.

2. Ibid., 28.

3. Ibid., 42.

4. Ibid., 88.

5. Author's interview with Dick Francis, London, 14 September 1983.

6. Dick Francis, *Blood Sport* (New York: Harper & Row, 1967), 6, 9. All page references throughout these notes relate to this edition.

7. Ibid., 59.

8. Ibid., 139.

9. Dick Francis, *Forfeit* (New York: Harper & Row, 1969), 124. All page references throughout these notes relate to this edition.

10. Ibid., 3.

11. Ibid., 23.

12. Ibid., 140.

13. Ibid., 179–180.

14. Ibid., 184.

5. The Hero as Victim, Pilot, and Son
Enquiry, Rat Race, Bonecrack

1. Dick Francis, *Enquiry* (New York: Harper & Row, 1970), 3. All page references throughout these notes relate to this edition.

2. Ibid., 100–101.

3. Ibid., 132.

4. Ibid., 120.

5. Ibid., 152.

6. Dick Francis, *Rat Race* (New York: Harper & Row, 1971), 3. All page references throughout these notes relate to this edition.

7. Ibid., 32.

8. Ibid., 49–50.

9. H. R. F. Keating, Review of *Rat Race*, *The Times* (29 October 1970), 14.

10. Francis, *Rat Race*, 82.

11. Dick Francis, *Bonecrack* (New York: Harper & Row, 1972), 1. All page references throughout these notes relate to this edition.

12. Ibid., 41.
13. Ibid., 42.
14. Ibid., 68.
15. Ibid., 76.
16. Ibid., 91.

6. The Hero as Movie Star, Detective, and Bloodstock Agent
Smokescreen, Slayride, Knockdown

1. Timothy Foote, "Reading and Riding," *Time* magazine (22 May 1972). Review of *Bonecrack*.
2. Dick Francis, *Smokescreen* (New York: Harper & Row, 1973), 54–55. All page references throughout these notes relate to this edition.
3. Ibid., 153–155.
4. Ibid., 131.
5. Dick Francis, *Slayride* (New York: Harper & Row, 1973), 68. All page references throughout these notes relate to this edition.
6. Ibid., 69.
7. Ibid., 98.
8. Ibid., 126.
9. Philip Pelham, Review of *Knock Down*, *London Magazine* 14, no.6 (February–March 1975): 142–143.
10. Dick Francis, *Knockdown* (New York: Harper & Row, 1975), 22–23. All page references throughout these notes relate to this edition.
11. Ibid., 193.

7. The Hero as Toymaker, Artist, and Accountant
High Stakes, In the Frame, Risk

1. Dick Francis, *High Stakes* (New York: Harper & Row, 1975), 17–18. All page references throughout these notes relate to this edition.
2. Ibid., 93.
3. Ibid., 135.
4. Joan B. Fiscella, "A Sense of the Under Toad: Play in Mystery Fiction," *Clues: a Journal of Detection* 1, #2 (Fall/Winter 1980), 1–7.

5. Author's interview with Dick Francis, London, 14 September 1983.

6. Dick Francis, *In the Frame* (New York: Harper & Row, 1977), 102.

7. Ibid.

8. Dick Francis, *Risk* (New York: Harper & Row, 1978), 56. All page references throughout these notes relate to this edition.

9. Ibid., 62.

10. Ibid., 66–67.

11. Alex de Jonge, "Toughs of the Turf," *The Times Literary Supplement* (28 October 1977), 1258. Review of *Risk*.

8. The Hero as Envoy, Photographer, and Duo
Trial Run, Reflex, Twice Shy

1. Dick Francis, *Trial Run* (New York: Harper & Row, 1979), 4. All page references throughout these notes relate to this edition.

2. Ibid., 12.

3. Ibid., 88.

4. Ibid., 139.

5. Ibid., 238.

6. Dick Francis, *Reflex* (New York: G. P. Putnam's Sons, 1981), 10–11. All page references throughout these notes relate to this edition.

7. Ibid., 25–26.

8. Ibid., 17–19.

9. Ibid., 59.

10. Carr, "Dick Francis," 205.

11. Dick Francis, *Twice Shy* (New York: G. P. Putnam's Sons, 1982), 117. All page references throughout these notes relate to this edition.

12. Ibid., 89.

13. Ibid., 177.

9. The Hero as Financier and Kidnap Consultant
Banker, The Danger

1. Eric Hiscock, "Book of the Month," *The Bookseller* (25 September 1982), 1201. Review of *Banker*.

2. Eric Hiscock, "Book of the Month," *The Bookseller* (1 October 1983), 1477. Review of *The Danger*.

3. Dick Francis, *Banker* (New York: Putnam, 1983), 18. All page references throughout these notes relate to this edition.

4. Ibid., 26.

5. Ibid., 30.

6. Ibid., 118.

7. Ibid., 215–216.

8. T. J. Binyon, "At Liberty and Not," *The Times Literary Supplement* (11 November 1983), 1255. Review of *The Danger*.

9. Dick Francis, *The Danger* (New York: Putnam, 1984), 27.

10. Winner's Enclosure

1. T. J. Binyon, Review of *Banker, The Times Literary Supplement* (10 December 1982), 1378.

2. Dudley Doust, "Francis: The Plot Thickens," *The Sunday Times* (20 December 1981), 21.

3. Philip Larkin, "Four Legs Good," *The Times Literary Supplement* (10 October 1980), 1127. Review of *Reflex*.

4. Author's interview with Dick Francis, London, 14 September 1983.

5. Newgate Callendar, "A Jockey Who Writes Winners," *The Dial* 2, #3 (March 1981), 8–9. Published by WNET/13, Public Broadcasting Communications Inc.

6. Carr, "Dick Francis," 205.

7. Heywood Hale Broun, "Dick Francis and the Racing Game," *The Washington Post Book World* (27 March 1983). Review of *Banker*.

8. Author's interview.

9. Snow, "Over the Sticks."

10. Author's interview.

11. Newgate Callendar, Review of *Trial Run, The New York Times Book Review* (20 May 1979), 34, 36.

12. John Welcome, "Under Pressure," *London Magazine* 19, #12 (March 1980), 95–96. Review of *Whip Hand*.

13. Author's interview.

14. Geoffrey Stokes, "Edmund Wilson was a Fuddy-duddy, or, Why I Like Dick Francis," *Village Voice* (27 June 1977).

15. Ibid.

16. Fred Erisman, "Crime Fiction: Some Varieties of Historical Experience," *Clues: A Journal of Detection* 1, #1 (Spring 1980), 1–8.

17. Michael N. Stanton, "Dick Francis: The Worth of Human Love," *The Armchair Detective* 15, #2 (1982), 137–143.

18. Author's interview.

19. Francis, *The Sport of Queens*, 238.

20. Author's interview.

21. H. R. F. Keating, "Dick Francis," in *Twentieth Century Crime and Mystery Writers*, edited by John M. Reilly (London: Macmillan, 1980; New York: St. Martin's Press, 1980).

22. Raymond Chandler, Introduction to *The Simple Art of Murder* (Boston: Houghton Mifflin, 1950; London: Hamish Hamilton, 1950).

23. Francis, *Forfeit*, 126–127.

24. Francis, *Banker*, 86.

25. Francis, *The Danger*, 98.

26. Francis, *Whip Hand*, 125.

27. Francis, *Blood Sport*, 160.

28. Francis, *Slayride*, 43.

29. Francis, *Knockdown*, 28.

30. Ibid., 190.

31. Francis, *Flying Finish*, 18.

32. Francis, *Trial Run*, 49.

33. Francis, *Smokescreen*, 155.

34. Francis, *Slayride*, 112.

35. Francis, *Banker*, 87.

36. Judith Rascoe, "On Vicarious Danger," *The Christian Science Monitor* (17 July 1969), 11. Review of *Forfeit*.

37. Francis, *Whip Hand*, 20–21.

38. Francis, *The Sport of Queens*, Third revised edition, 244–245. Jane McLoughlin, "Mary's Job: Getting the Jockey to his Mount on Time," *Daily Telegraph* (12 May 1973), 14.

39. Mary Francis, *The Beginner's Guide to Flying* (London: Pelham Books,

1969). Revised as *Flying Start: A Guide to Flying Light Aircraft* (London: Pelham Books, 1980).

40. Julian Symons, Review of *Reflex*, *The New York Times Book Review* (29 March 1981), 3, 45.

41. Stanton, "Dick Francis: The Worth of Human Love."

42. Francis, *Nerve*, 187.

43. Dick Francis, "Belief is a Computer," *Sunday Telegraph Magazine* (19 February 1978).

44. Edmund Crispin, "Global Consequences of Murder Most Horrible," *The Sunday Times* (24 October 1976), 41. Review of *In the Frame*.

45. Snow, "Over the Sticks."

46. Philip Larkin, Review of *Banker*, *The Observer* (17 October 1982).

Bibliography

1. Works by Dick Francis

A. Novels

Dead Cert. London: Michael Joseph, 1962. New York: Holt Rinehart, 1962.

Nerve. London: Michael Joseph, 1964. New York: Harper, 1964.

For Kicks. London: Michael Joseph, 1965. New York: Harper, 1965.

Odds Against. London: Michael Joseph, 1965. New York: Harper, 1966.

Flying Finish. London: Michael Joseph, 1966. New York: Harper, 1967.

Blood Sport. London: Michael Joseph, 1967. New York: Harper, 1968.

Forfeit. London: Michael Joseph, 1968. New York: Harper, 1969.

Enquiry. London: Michael Joseph, 1969. New York: Harper, 1970.

Rat Race. London: Michael Joseph, 1970. New York: Harper, 1971.

Bonecrack. London: Michael Joseph, 1971. New York: Harper, 1972.

Smokescreen. London: Michael Joseph, 1972. New York: Harper, 1973.

Slay-Ride. London: Michael Joseph, 1973. *Slayride*. New York: Harper, 1974.

Knock Down. London: Michael Joseph, 1974. *Knockdown*. New York: Harper, 1975.

High Stakes. London: Michael Joseph, 1975. New York: Harper, 1976.

In the Frame. London: Michael Joseph, 1976. New York: Harper, 1977.

Risk. London: Michael Joseph, 1977. New York: Harper, 1978.

Trial Run. London: Michael Joseph, 1978. New York: Harper, 1979.

Whip Hand. London: Michael Joseph, 1979. New York: Harper, 1980.

Reflex. London: Michael Joseph, 1980. New York: Putnam, 1981.

Twice Shy. London: Michael Joseph, 1981. New York: Putnam, 1982.

Banker. London: Michael Joseph, 1982. New York: Putnam, 1983.

The Danger. London: Michael Joseph, 1983. New York: Putnam, 1984.

Proof. London: Michael Joseph, 1984. New York: Putnam, 1985.

Break In. London: Michael Joseph, 1985. New York: Putnam, 1986.

B. Uncollected Short Stories

Note: "Dead Cert" and "The Midwinter Gold Cup" are edited excerpts from the novels *Dead Cert* and *Nerve* respectively. The earliest original short story is therefore "Carrot for a Chestnut." Each story is cited here as follows: first British publication, followed by first US publication (or vice versa if it appeared first in the USA); first British publication in an anthology, followed by first US publication in an anthology (or vice versa if anthologized first in the USA); alternative titles for the story, similarly arranged. Each distinct story is numbered for easy reference.

1. "Dead Cert." In *Best Racing and Chasing Stories*, edited by Dick Francis and John Welcome. London: Faber, 1966.

2. "The Midwinter Gold Cup." In *Best Racing and Chasing Stories 2*, edited by Dick Francis and John Welcome. London: Faber, 1969.

3. "Carrot for a Chestnut." *Sports Illustrated* 32 (5 January 1970), 48–59. *Argosy* 31, #5 (May 1970), 40–58. In *The Welcome Collection: Fourteen Racing Stories*, edited by John Welcome. London: Michael Joseph, 1972. *Stories of Crime and Detection*, edited by Joan D. Berbrich. New York: McGraw-Hill, 1974.

4. "A Day of Wine and Roses." *Sports Illustrated* 38 (7 May 1973), 106–112.

   A.k.a. "The Gift." In *Winter's Crimes 5*, edited by Virginia Whitaker. London: Macmillan, 1973.

A.k.a. "The Big Story." *Ellery Queen's Mystery Magazine* No. 373 (December 1974). In *Ellery Queen's Crime Wave*, edited by Ellery Queen. New York: Putnam, 1976. London: Gollancz, 1976.

5. "Nightmare." *The Times* (13 April 1974), 7. *Ellery Queen's Mystery Magazine* #379 (June 1975). In *Ellery Queen's Searches and Seizures*, edited by Ellery Queen. New York: Davis, 1977. *John Creasey's Crime Collection 1977*, edited by Herbert Harris. London: Gollancz, 1977.

6. "The Rape of Kingdom Hill." *The Times* (25 October 1975), 6.

   A.k.a. "The Royal Ripoff at Kingdom Hill." *Classic Magazine* (June–July 1976).

7. "The Day of the Losers." *Horse and Hound* (4 February 1977), 8–11. *Ellery Queen's Mystery Magazine* No.457 (September 1981). In *John Creasey's Crime Collection 1980*, edited by Herbert Harris. London: Gollancz, 1980.

   A.k.a. "Fix the National!" Parts 1, 2. *Daily Star* (29 March, 30 March 1979).

8. "Twenty-one Good Men and True." In *Verdict of Thirteen: a Detection Club Anthology*, edited by Julian Symons. London: Faber, 1979. New York: Harper, 1979.

   A.k.a. "Blind Chance." *Woman's Own* (25 August 1979).

9. "Bright White Star." *Cheshire Life* (Christmas 1979).

   A.k.a. "A Bright Star in a Dirty World." *Pacemaker's Racing Digest* (Winter 1980).

10. "Two to One Against." *Woman's Own* (26 January 1980).

    A.k.a. "Spring Fever." Parts 1, 2. *Horse and Rider* 30, #s 348, 349 (February, March 1981).

C. Other Works

The Sport of Queens: The Autobiography of Dick Francis. London: Michael Joseph, 1957. Third revised edition, 1982. New York: Harper, 1969.

Best Racing and Chasing Stories, edited by Dick Francis and John Welcome. London: Faber, 1966.

Best Racing and Chasing Stories 2, edited by Dick Francis and John Welcome. London: Faber, 1969.

The Racing Man's Bedside Book, edited by Dick Francis and John Welcome. London: Faber, 1969.

2. Works about Francis

"Authors and Editors." *Publishers Weekly* 193 (8 January 1968), 27–28.

Axthelm, Pete. "Writer with a Whip Hand." *Newsweek* 97 (6 April 1981), 98, 100.

Bauska, Barry. "Endure and Prevail: the Novels of Dick Francis." *The Armchair Detective* 11, #3 (July 1978), 238–244.

Bishop, Paul. "The Sport of Sleuths." *The Armchair Detective* 17, #2 (Spring 1984), 144–147. This is an updated and expanded version of material which first appeared in *The Thieftaker Journals* 2, #4 (May 1983).

Breen, Jon L. "Breakneck." Short story. *Ellery Queen's Mystery Magazine* #351 (February 1973). In *Hair of the Sleuth-Hound: Parodies of Mystery Fiction*, by Jon L. Breen. Metuchen, N.J.: Scarecrow Press, 1982.

Burnet, Alistair. "Straight from the Horse's Mouth." *The Listener* 92 (22 August 1974), 235–237.

Callendar, Newgate. "A Jockey Who Writes Winners." *The Dial* 2, #3 (March 1981), 8–9. Published by WNET/13, Public Broadcasting Communications Inc.

Cantwell, Robert. "Mystery Makes a Writer." *Sports Illustrated* 28 (25 March 1968), 76–88.

Carr, John C. "Dick Francis." In *The Craft of Crime: Conversations with Crime Writers*, by John C. Carr. Boston: Houghton Mifflin, 1983.

Cooper-Clark, Diana. "Interview with Dick Francis." In *Designs of Darkness: Interviews with Detective Novelists*, by Diana Cooper-Clark. Bowling Green, Ohio: Bowling Green State University Popular Press, 1983. Also slightly edited as "Hoof-beats and Heroes: an Interview with Dick Francis." *London Magazine* 23, #8 (November 1983), 58–70.

"Dick Francis." *The New Yorker* 45 (15 March 1969), 29–30. "Talk of the Town" interview.

Doyle, Katie. "He Still Finds the Winners!" *Manchester Evening News* (4 November 1982). Light article.

Durrant, Digby. "Born Winner." *London Magazine* 14, #2 (June/July 1974), 90–93.

Fitzgeorge-Parker, Tim. *Steeplechase Jockeys: The Great Ones*. London: Pelham Books, 1971.

Flor, Dorothy-Anne. "Beyond the Finish Line." *Shoreline* (17 April 1983). Supplement to *Fort Lauderdale News and Sun-Sentinel*.

Fox, James. "Paperback Rider." *Sunday Times Magazine* (10 September 1972), 37–38, 41.

Garner, Lesley. "The Best-selling Passions of Mary Francis." *The Mail on Sunday* (10 October 1982), 17. Describes the support and technical research given by Dick's wife Mary.

Gott, Shirley. "Jockey Dick's Written Plenty of Winners." *New Reveille* (5 October 1973), 13. Light article.

Harvey, Eleanor. "Me and my Marriage, by Dick Francis." *Woman's Own* (25 August 1979), 12–13. Light article.

Hughes, David. "A Lucky Craftsman." *Books and Bookmen* (October 1982), 26–27.

Keating, H. R. F. "Dick Francis." In *Twentieth Century Crime and Mystery Writers*, edited by John M. Reilly. London: Macmillan, 1980. New York: St. Martin's Press, 1980.

Kendall, Ena. "A Room of my Own: Dick Francis." *Observer Magazine* (28 August 1983), 28–29. Light article.

Lloyd, Simon. "Mystery of Piggott's Biographer is Solved: It's Dick Francis." Baltimore: *The Horsemen's Journal* (November 1981), 32–34.

Lord, Graham. "The Amazing Woman Dick Francis Married." *Sunday Express* (3 August 1980), 6. Light article.

Mills, Nancy. "The Winning Partnership of Dick and Mary Francis." *Woman's Realm* 33, no.995 (2 July 1977), 12–13, 15. Light article.

———. "In the Winner's Circle with the Queen Mother." *New York Daily News* (13 November 1977). Light article.

Mortimer, John. "Don't Give me Shakespeare! Interviews with Dick Francis and Catherine Cookson." *Sunday Times* (15 August 1982), 25. Also slightly expanded in *In Character*, by John Mortimer. London: Allen Lane, 1983.

Newcombe, J. "Close-up: Jockey with an Eye for Intrigue." *Life* 66 (6 June 1969), 81–82.

Nicholson, Geoffrey. "Tales of the Turf." *Observer Magazine* (30 September 1979), 60–63.

Patience, Sally. "Dick Francis . . . a Full Life." *Woman and Home* (April 1975), 58–60. Light article.

"Riding High." *Forbes* 117 (15 April 1976), 100. Published by *Forbes*, 60 Fifth Avenue, New York, NY 10011.

Snow, C. P. "Over the Sticks." *Financial Times* (19 July 1973), 33.

Stanton, Michael N. "Dick Francis: The Worth of Human Love." *The Armchair Detective* 15, #2 (1982), 137–143.

Stokes, Geoffrey. "Edmund Wilson was a Fuddy-duddy, or, Why I Like Dick Francis." *Village Voice* (27 June 1977).

Thornton, Gillian. "21 Again!" *Annabel* (November 1982), 5–6. Light article; the title refers to the fact that *Banker*, just published, was Francis's twenty-first novel published twenty-one years after he began his first.

Zuckerman, Edward. "The Winning Form of Dick Francis." *The New York Times Magazine* (25 March 1984), 40 ff.

Index